dinofile

dinofile

Profiles of 120 amazing,
terrifying and bizarre beasts

Professor Richard Moody

hamlyn

First published in Great Britain in 2006 by Hamlyn,
a division of Octopus Publishing Group Ltd
2–4 Heron Quays, London E14 4JP

The right of Richard Moody to be identified as
the author of this work has been asserted by
him in accordance with the Copyright,
Designs and Patents Act, 1988.

Distributed in the United States and Canada by
Sterling Publishing Co., Inc.
387 Park Avenue South,
New York,NY 10016-8810

ISBN-13: 978-0-600-61400-5
ISBN-10: 0-600-61400-X

A CIP catalogue record for this book
is available from the British Library

Printed and bound in China

10 9 8 7 6 5 4 3 2 1

CONTENTS

Introduction

Dinosaurs are the one link that most of us have with the wonderful science of geology (the study of the structure of the Earth). Earthquakes, volcanoes and tsunamis (gigantic waves) are other phenomena that reveal the workings of our planet but dinosaurs have a 'wow!' factor that attracts people of all ages. My own interest began as a university student. I was fortunate to have won-derful teachers who stimulated my mind and introduced me to the ideas of geological time and evolution and taught me how to observe, record and interpret.

New discoveries

In my student days, dinosaurs had a reputation for being heavy, cumbersome creatures that roamed slowly across a world populated by primitive mammals and non-flowering plants. However, new discoveries and the advancement of science resulted in massive changes in the way that we interpreted dinosaur movement and the relationships that existed in dinosaur communities, worldwide.

Reliable four-wheel-drive vehicles, cheap air travel and easy access to previously exotic regions enabled dinosaur palaeontologists (scientists who study fossils) to explore new areas. As a result, numerous world-class sites have been found in Asia, South America and Australia since the early 1960s. Thanks also to a better understanding of the established sites of the USA, Canada and Eurasia, our knowledge of dinosaurs has grown enormously. Great debates on the warm- or cold-blooded theory and the links between birds and dinosaurs have dominated our science over the last three decades ,but the discoveries of feathered dinosaurs, embryos and, most recently, soft tissues have stimu-lated a renewed interest in the 'Terrible Lizards'.

Recent find
The remains of *Falcarius*, a medium-size theropod, were found in 2005.

Research and exploration

My own interests in palaeontology (which is Latin for 'the study of prehistoric beings') parallel the developments of the last 30 or 40 years. Teaching, research and exploration have marked a lifetime absorbed by my science and I will always cherish the days when we loaded up an assortment of vehicles to explore areas of Europe or North Africa under the blazing summer sun. In due course my expeditions extended further afield, reaching out to Nigeria, Niger and Mali in West Africa. We explored huge landscapes, learned how to survive and how to cook. We could spend weeks without washing but the intro-duction of wet wipes and ceramic water filters made desert life tolerable.

Hardships were to be endured but the discovery of the first fossil, hundreds of miles away from the nearest house, eliminated any doubts as to why we were doing this. Imagine finding perfectly preserved fish, ghost shrimps, crocodile teeth and a host of seashells, sea urchins and numerous sea turtles on the edge of the Sahara Desert. Think of the desert as an inland sea 120 million years ago and you will realize that geology and palaeontology are live sciences full of facts, theories and explanations. In Niger we went on to find numerous skeletons of sauropod dinosaurs and the teeth of carnivores. The desert wastes of central and eastern Niger were once the home of *Ouranosaurus*, *Spinosaurus*, *Afrovenator* and *Jobaria*, alongside the 'supercroc' *Suchomimus*.

Friends and I have walked in search of dinosaurs and thoroughly enjoyed a life of close friendships, discovery and the knowledge that every day we were learning something new, including how to raise water from a desert well and negotiate our way out of jail!

Introduction

Cousins
Alioramus was a relative of the giant meat eaters such as *Tarbosaurus* from Mongolia.

Dinosaurs discovered!

Richard Owen
Sir Richard Owen photographed along-with the skeleton of an extinct giant *Moa*.

Few animals, living or extinct, are as interesting as dinosaurs. The word 'dinosaur' comes from two Greek words: *deinos* (meaning 'terrible') and *sauros* (meaning 'lizard'). Richard Owen (1804–92) was a famous anatomist (an expert in the structure of humans and animals) and he first used the word to describe the bones of three unique but related fossil reptiles found in southern England. In 1841 he revealed to an unsuspecting world that a unique 'tribe' of giant, four-legged reptiles had once roamed our planet. Robert Plot (1640–96) had first recorded gigantic fossilized bones in 1677, but at the time scientists thought that they belonged to a huge man. Richard Owen's announcement was based on the fossilized bones of *Megalosaurus* (see page 51), *Hylaeosaurus* (see page 94) and *Iguanodon* (see page 106).

A major science

The study of dinosaurs is called palaeontology. By the early 19th century, geology , palaeontology and anatomy were major sciences of the day, and doctors, clergymen and members of the general public all searched quarries and coastlines for fossils. The bones of *Iguanodon* were first discovered in 1809 in south-east England, near Cuckfield, East Sussex. Professor the Reverend William Buckland (1754–1856) found those of *Megalosaurus* near Stonesfield in north Oxfordshire in 1818, and gave it its name in 1824. *Iguanodon* and *Hylaeosaurus* were given their names in 1825 and 1833 respectively by the geologist and palaeontologist, Gideon Mantell (1790–1852). Neither man realized the importance of his findings. It was left to Owen to establish a new 'tribe' or order of reptiles – the Dinosauria.

Recent advances

Since those heady early days of exciting finds, our knowledge of dinosaurs has increased dramatically, with the discovery of around 750 species of dinosaur worldwide. New skeletal material has revealed a diverse array of animals adapted to a wide range of ecological niches (particular environ-ments). Some discoveries are not even of the fossilized hard parts of these prehistoric creatures. The most recent advances involve detailed studies of eggs, embryos and soft tissue. I repeat, *soft tissue*! This includes bone cells, blood vessels and possibly even blood cells. One day we may be able to analyse dinosaur DNA.

Once upon a time in the West

During the second half of the 19th century the search for dinosaurs centred on North America, with Joseph Leidy, Othniel Charles Marsh, Edward Drinker Cope, Earl Douglass and Joseph Tyrell discovering dozens of new dinosaurs and hundreds of tonnes of bones in Montana, New Jersey, Colorado, Wyoming, New Mexico and Alberta. Over a 50-year period the rivalry between individual dinosaur hunters reached a near warlike fever pitch. This was all the more remarkable because Cope and his professional fossil hunter Charles Hazelius Sternberg, began digging for dinosaurs in Montana in 1876, just after the great Sioux warrior Sitting Bull had wiped out Lieutenant-Colonel George Armstrong Custer and 263 others at the Battle of the Little Big Horn.

In the early 1900s Earl Douglass found the incredibly rich dinosaur deposits of the Uinta Mountains in Utah, which later became the Dinosaur National Monument. In 1910 Barnum Brown also discovered lots of remains in deposits left by the Red Deer River across the Canadian border in Alberta.

By the 1920s dinosaur hunts had turned up significant finds in Africa and Central Asia, with Roy Chapman Andrews leading four expeditions into the Gobi Desert. It is now claimed that a new dinosaur is found every seven weeks, and there is little else to compare with the heart-pumping thrill of finding a 20-m-long (65 ft) monster. Great dinosaur discoveries have been made recently on the edges of the Sahara Desert; in the badlands of Argentina; in Queensland, Australia; and especially in China. Gigantic sauropods, feathered dinosaurs and the skeletons of unborn baby dinosaurs reveal more and more about the world of the 'terrible lizards'.

Discoveries such as the blood cells and soft tissue in a Tyrannosaurus (see page 64) limb bone from the Hell Creek Formation of Montana bring us even closer to resolving the links between dinosaurs and birds.

Early collection
Barnum Brown with dinosaur bones from Big Horn, Wyoming, USA, safely wrapped in plaster jackets.

Introduction

A long, long time ago

The first dinosaurs appeared approximately 230 million years ago and the last disappeared 164.5 million years later at the end of the Cretaceous period of the Mesozoic era. The demise of the dinosaurs heralded the beginning of the Age of Mammals (Cenozoic era) some 65.5 million years ago.

From around 6 million years ago to the present day, about 15 species of hominids (human-like mammals) have come and, mostly, gone. Compare this with the dinosaurs. After 165 million years of world domination, the dinosaur family tree as we know it now, contains around 540 dinosaur genera and 750 species and there may be another 700 genera waiting to be found!

During the Middle Triassic period, some 220 million years ago, plant-eating dinosaurs (herbivores) and meat eaters (carnivores) appeared and, at almost the same time, four-footed and two-footed forms (quadrupeds and bipeds) also evolved. The dinosaurs were derived from the so-called 'tooth in socket' reptiles, the thecodonts, which lived during Permian and Triassic times.

There is little doubt that the dinosaurs were an evolutionary success story. But, as scientists, we should ask why. Reptiles were better adapted to life on land than amphibians (frogs and toads). They had a scaly skin and laid shelled eggs with an internal food supply (yolk) that protected and nourished the embryo until it was time for it to hatch.

Dinosaurs had an upright stance with their limbs drawn underneath the body. Interestingly, the more the dinosaur evolved, the fewer digits it seems to have had on the ends of those limbs. They could probably move more quickly than their immediate competitors and, if they were warm-blooded and had four-chambered hearts, as some scientists think they did, then they would have been better able to survive on land than any other group apart from the emerging mammals. Surprisingly, the mammals had to wait 170 million years before conditions were right for their success.

The changing shape of continents

Climate, plant life and the shape of the land (topography) probably influenced the success of the dinosaurs. Over 240 million years ago, most of the continents were one, the super-continent that we call Pangaea. The climate was hot and dry almost everywhere and the plant cover was changing from club mosses and tree ferns to primitive conifers, ferns and cycads (seed-bearing palm-like trees). By 225 million years ago these plants were common along river channels and across flood plains, and it is likely that prosauropods such as *Plateosaurus* (see page 20) and small theropods such as *Compsognathus* (see page 58) lived in such environments.

By the end of the Triassic period, 200 million years ago, Pangaea had started to break up. Around 190 million years ago, a huge meteorite hit the Earth in an area that is now Quebec in Canada, and this may have caused the extinction of a number of species around the world. Many dinosaurs survived, however, to thrive in the cooler, wetter climates of the Jurassic period (200–145 million years ago). Ginkgos and monkey-puzzle-like conifers formed an important part of the Jurassic flora (plant life), together with early pines, ferns and cycads. In some areas there is evidence of seasons.

From outer space, planet Earth would have begun to look much greener as thousands of plants spread across the planet to diminish the area where arid conditions once prevailed. The Jurassic landscape was home to a host of dinosaurs, including giant plant eaters, meat eaters, scavengers and nest robbers.

Different areas of this new world bred different dinosaur communities. However, the fact that some sorts of dinosaurs were spread across the world shows that migration between widely separated areas was still possible. The seas of the Jurassic era were dominated by the fish-like ichthyosaurs and short-necked, paddle-limbed plesiosaurs, while the flying lizards, the pterosaurs, ruled the skies. The first bird, *Archaeopteryx* (see page 115), appeared during Late Jurassic times in the area that we now know as southern Germany.

The breakup of the continents continued throughout the Cretaceous period (145–65.5 million years ago). The changing climate brought with it warm, humid conditions and, though conifers, ferns and cycads dominated the plant life of the Early Cretaceous, there were local variations in floras where drier conditions occurred in the uplands. By the end of the Cretaceous, flowering plants were becoming a major component of the world's vegetation and many of these plants may have been poisonous to dinosaurs and other animals.

During the Cretaceous, the rise of the ornithopod dinosaurs such as *Hypsilophodon* (see page 103) and the duck-billed hadrosaurs shows there was a great change in dinosaur communities. The sauropods were in decline. Armoured dinosaurs evolved thicker scales to defend themselves against giants such as *Tarbosaurus* (see page 63), *Tyrannosaurus* (see page 64) and *Albertosaurus*. Feathered, bird-like dinosaurs seem now to have become an important component of some Late Cretaceous communities. Indeed, the discovery of blood vessels and bone cells has now more or less proved that there is a direct link between today's birds and certain dinosaurs. And during the Mesozoic, the food chains or webs were invariably dominated by the biggest meat eaters, in the same way that the top predators on the African savannas today are the big cats, such as the lions.

At the end of the Cretaceous period the combination of continental separation, climatic variation, faster changes in vegetation, mountain building, exceptional volcanic activity and the coming of a huge meteor strike in the Gulf of Mexico proved too much for many forms of life, including the dinosaurs. The mass extinctions of the Late Cretaceous also saw the demise of the ichthyosaurs, plesiosaurs, mosasaurs and pterosaurs. The new world of the Cenozoic era was to be ruled by mammals and birds, and flowering plants included grasses and sea-grasses.

The rise of the ornithopods
Hypsilophodon was a primitive ornithopod from the Early Cretaceous.

How are fossils formed?

The earliest fossils occur in rocks laid down on the surface of our planet approximately 3.5 billion years ago. They are the remains of primitive organisms that mark the origins of life on Earth. There are fossils of single- and multi-celled organisms, but you usually need a research microscope to see them. In Shark Bay, Western Australia, fossil mounds occur in the tidal zone, so they are uncovered daily. This exposes the structures to extreme changes in environment and suggests that they are robustly built.

The mounds are made by sand grains that gather on the surface of a sticky mat made of algae. Each layer is a new period of grain accumulation. The resulting mound is therefore a support structure for the organism. As each new layer of algae is formed, the one beneath does not survive. It would also die if it was buried rapidly under an accumulation of sand, limestone or mudstone. The robust nature of the 'skeleton' would probably allow it to survive, however, and such structures have proved durable worldwide, for billions of years.

Of course, many fossil algal mounds will have been destroyed as a result of erosion or the many other physical and chemical processes that have occurred naturally throughout Earth's long history. More delicate organisms, without shells or skeletons, are even less likely to have survived fossilization and be preserved. The fossil record is very incomplete and the vast majority of soft-bodied organisms leave no trace of their existence.

Where there is evidence of soft-bodied creatures or delicate plant material, it is often found in fine-grained rocks, such as mudstones, siltstones or limestones. Many of these are laid down in water. The fossils of soft-bodied organisms are invariably impressions, casts and moulds, frequently etched by a thin mineral deposit. Such delicate traces and fine sediments suggest a quick, quiet burial, the absence of oxygen and a lack of scavengers.

There was no oxygen in the Earth's early atmosphere. If it had been present, then oxidation would have inhibited the vital processes that led to the origins of life. An oxygen-free (anoxic) environment inhibits the activity of bacteria and prevents decay.

About 600 million years ago, organisms with supportive and protective skeletons began to

Fossils
The mineralized shells of ammonites are frequently found in rocks laid down in Mesozoic oceans.

appear in the fossil record. The skeletons of early organisms usually formed on the outside of the plant or animal, but gradually more complex internal skeletons evolved as the variety of life increased. Animals and plants use a different number of minerals and chemical compounds to build their hard parts. These include aragonite, calcite, silica and calcium phosphate (bone).

So the preservation of skeletal hard parts relies on rapid burial and the absence of scavengers, but by the beginning of the Palaeozoic era (542–251 million years ago) the chances of fossilization increased dramatically and so we are much more likely to discover a representative of an ancient community from that time onwards.

The mineral remains of organisms are often altered through time, with new minerals replacing old. This process might occur because mineral-rich waters have passed through rocks. Original skeletons are often dissolved in acidic waters. When this happens, the space that remains acts as a natural mould that can be filled by new minerals to give casts of the original.

Tracks, trails, burrows and borings are also evidence of life, and these trace fossils can provide detailed information on locomotion (movement) or lifestyle. Dinosaur footprints and trail-ways provide data on the size, form and, most interestingly, the pace or speed at which the animal walked or ran! All types of fossils are important clues to the history of life on Earth.

In death
The skeletons of *Oviraptor* and *Protoceratops,* buried together by a sand storm.

How dinosaurs are classified

Classification is essentially the study of the natural relationships between groups of living things. It is based on the detailed analysis of similarities and differences; organisms that are the least similar to one another are likely to be more distantly related than those that are more similar and have evolved along different paths.

Understanding classification

Let us take you, the reader, as an example! You are a human being, a hominid. Every person you know or meet is an intelligent creature and is a member of the human species, that is, *Homo sapiens*. This name is derived from the two Latin words *homo* (human) and *sapiens* (wise).

If you travelled back in time 40,000 years, however, you would be likely to meet a relatively close ancestor, *Homo neanderthalis*, Neanderthal man. The name clearly indicates that this hominid belongs to the same genus but to a different species. The two of you would share many characteristics but the Neanderthal would be shorter and stockier, with a prominent jaw, larger teeth and strongly developed ridges above the eyes.

Go back several million years and your ancestors, found in areas such as Kenya and Ethiopia, would be capable of walking upright but they would be more ape-like in their general appearance. These creatures would belong to a different genus, and scientists have used names such as *Australopithecus anamensis* to describe one of the first creatures of our family tree. The name literally means the 'southern ape of the lake'.

Life on Earth reaches back 3.5 billion years. Within that time-span the number of new species is simply phenomenal and it is essential to organize them if we are to understand the process and progress of evolution. If we repeatedly used the same name we would have chaos!

The branches of your family tree can be compared with the trees in your local park, with the oldest branches at the bottom. The number of branches and side-branches or offshoots will depend on the age of the tree, and the oldest tree represents a complex history over a long period of time. It is the same with the dinosaurs.

To rationalize the relationships of organisms on a broader scale, several genera are grouped together to form a family. One or more families are referred to an order and orders are grouped together into classes. Classes are grouped into phyla and phyla into kingdoms. Other groups and subgroups may also be used. While there may be millions of species, there are just five kingdoms. They are:

• Plants
• Animals
• Fungi
• Bacteria
• Single-celled animals (Protoctists)

The state of dinosaur classification is continually changing, often as a result of the computerized sorting of individual characteristics. Different workers place different emphasis on different characteristics and, although the overall 'tree' may remain much the same, a known species may sometimes move its position to a different branch. Cladistics is the name given to the method of classification that most scientists prefer today. It is based on shared characteristics.

An example of a relatively detailed classification
can be based around *Tyrannosaurus rex.*

Rank	Name	Definition
Species	rex	king
Genus	Tyrannosaurus	tyrant lizard
Family	Tyrannosauridae	all family names end in *-idae*
Group	Tetanurae	Contains: Tyrannosauridae, Ornithomimidae Troodontidae, Coeluridae
Suborder	Theropoda	beast-footed dinosaurs Contains: all dinosaurs referred to as coelurosaurs and carnosaurs
Order	Saurischia	lizard-hipped dinosaurs theropods and sauropods
Subclass	Dinosauria	advanced reptiles with limbs drawn beneath the body, four-chambered heart
Class	Archosauria	reptiles with shared skull characteristics Includes: dinosaurs, pterosaurs, thecodonts and crocodiles
Subphylum	Vertebrata	animals with backbones
Phylum	Chordata	animals with nerve cord
Kingdom	Animalia	all animals

Introduction

Dinosaur families

Archaeopteryx
'Ancient Feather' was the first representative of the birds –
was it a living dinosaur?

This is a book of dinosaur facts. It is like a field guide on plants or animals, except that there are no living dinosaurs left on Earth. Just imagine a time when dinosaurs roamed our planet in large numbers – some of them meat eaters and some plant eaters. Holidays to Africa, Asia or North America in those days (225–655 million years ago) would have involved watching groups of *T. rex* instead of a pride of lions, or a herd of stegosaurs rather than zebras!

We might have judged them to be dinosaurs on the basis of the general shape of their bodies and then put them in separate groups because *T.rex* had two legs and the stegosaurs walked on all fours. As we got closer to the animals in both groups, we would see differences within the same group, perhaps in the teeth or the numbers of fingers and toes. With these differences in mind, we could break up our two groups even more and create a chart which recorded the groups, families within those groups and individual species.

Unfortunately there are over 65 families of dinosaurs identified by experts, with many members of individual families known from a limited range of bone material. So palaeontologists have had to define dinosaurs using more detailed information. This book introduces you to over 40 of these families and the descriptions of each animal also outline the main features of its family. Instead of being divided into two-legged and four-legged animals, all the families belong to one of two main groups or orders: the lizard-hipped Saurischia or the bird-hipped Ornithischia.

The members of these orders can be identified only from their skeletons and our observations would therefore have to be undertaken in a museum or at a dinosaur dig.

If we continue with *T. rex* and the stegosaurs as our examples, *T. rex* was a lizard-hipped dinosaur and the stegosaurs were bird-hipped dinosaurs, the first having a four-pronged arrangement of the hip bones and the latter having a three-pronged arrangement. The hip of birds evolved separately.

Both lizard-hipped and bird-hipped dinosaurs can then be subdivided into groups or suborders.

Focusing on the *T.rex*. As a lizard-hipped dinosaur, the 'Tyrant Lizard' was a cousin of the sauropods. However, the skeletons show that it was also a fierce, fast-moving meat eater, which makes it a member of the suborder Theropoda. It is distinctly related to birds.

T. rex has also been linked with some of the most specialized forms of two-legged, meat-eating dinosaurs under the group name Tetanurae. Of these it is closer to members of Coelurosauria, a group of dinosaurs that varied a lot in terms of size and feeding habits, but shared features such as bird-like feet and large eyes.

Finally we arrive at the features that define the Tyrannosauridae, including huge heads, powerful jaws, large saw-edged teeth and small, muscular arms. *T. rex* was probably the most powerful of these giant killing machines and the name *Tyrannosaurus* (Tyrant Lizard) *rex* (King) was well chosen.

Throughout this book we have set out the Order, Suborder, Group, Family and other levels to which each of our dinosaurs belongs. Using the descriptions as a means of identification and recognition, you will be able to determine which animal belongs to which group on your next museum expedition. For example, in this book your reference to *T. rex* starts:

Latin or proper name Tyrannosaurus
Pronunciation Tie-ran-oh-saw-rus
Common name Tyrant Lizard
Information about different levels
ORDER **Saurischia**
SUBORDER **Theropoda**
GROUP **Tetanurae**
FAMILY **Tyrannosauridae**

'Tyrant Lizard King'
Tyrannosaurus rex was top of the food chain 70 million years ago.

How to use this book

Introduction

The book is organized by the Latin name of each dinosaur.

Each entry also includes the common name.

Use the quick-reference section to learn the key facts about each creature.

A question mark before a fact, such as a date, means that the information is doubtful.

Amazingly realistic illustrations show you what the dinosaur may have looked like.

Theropods

42 Gasosaurus gaz-oh-saw-rus

Gas Lizard

Saurischia • Theropoda • Neotheropoda • ?Tetanurae • Family: uncertain

FIRST DESCRIBED 1985 • FOUND Asia: China • LENGTH c.4 m (13 ft) • WEIGHT 150 kg (330 lb) • FOOD Meat

YOUNG Eggs • LIVED Late Jurassic 161-146 million years ago

The remains of *Gasosaurus* were discovered by the Chinese expert, Professor Dong Zhiming (1937–), who is often described as the 'world's greatest dinosaur hunter'. Professor Dong has found over a hundred dinosaur skeletons. His first finds were in 1963. He has devoted his life to studying fossilized backboned animals (vertebrate palaeontology), and seems to enjoy naming the dinosaurs he often unearths in his beloved country.

The full name of this medium-sized meat eater is *Gasosaurus constructus* because it was found on the gas and oil company construction site in Dashanpu. There is not enough material to place the 'Gas Lizard' in a particular family.

No skull fragments have been found up to now of *Gasosaurus*. It is usually illustrated, however, as a very fierce-looking theropod that attacked its prey in small groups. It is supposed to have had a large head and many sharp, saw-edged teeth. None of this can be confirmed at the present time, but it does show that, for dinosaurs at least, art sometimes overtakes science.

Ceratosaurus ser-ah-toe-saw-rus 43

Horned Lizard

Saurischia • Theropoda • Neotheropoda • Family: Ceratosauridae

FIRST DESCRIBED 1884 • FOUND North America: USA; Africa • LENGTH c.6 m (20 ft) • WEIGHT 1 t
• FOOD Meat • YOUNG Eggs • LIVED Late Jurassic–Early Cretaceous 161–140 million years ago

Ceratosaurus was a medium-sized theropod with a large head sporting a horn above the nose. It also had massive dagger-like teeth. It was first found in the western part of North America and lived at the same time as *Allosaurus* (see page 53). In fact, the bones of both dinosaurs have been found in the same quarry!

Described by the American palaeontologist, Othniel C. Marsh (1832–99), in 1884, *Ceratosaurus* was at first thought to have been a good swimmer, and to have used its long, thin tail to propel it through the water. This is extremely unlikely, however, as Ceratosaurus was quite heavily built and had short arms and powerful legs. It was, in fact, a fast runner and caught and killed its prey by crushing them in its massive, strong jaws. In comparison with *Allosaurus*, *Ceratosaurus* was a small but well-equipped rival.

Ceratosaurus had a horn on its nose. It also had two smaller horns over its eyebrows and some people think that together these provided protection in battle. Others think that the nasal horn was for display in dominant males. *Ceratosaurus* has been found in Utah and Colorado in the United States and Tanzania in East Africa.

Theropods

Introduction

Learn how to pronounce the Latin names of the dinosaurs.

Understand the order, sub-order, group and family names for each creature.

Discover fascinating facts about every dinosaur.

Scientific name – generic and specific – are always printed in italics.

Silhouettes provide an easy way to compare the size of the dinosaurs. Each creature is set against a person who is 2 m (6 ft) tall.

Plateosaurus plat-ee-oh-saw-rus
Flat Lizard

Saurischia • Sauropodomorpha • Prosauropoda • Family: Plateosauridae

FIRST DISCOVERED **1837** • FOUND **Europe: Germany, France, Switzerland** • LENGTH *c.***9 m (29½ ft)** • WEIGHT **4 t** • FOOD **Plants** • YOUNG **Eggs** • LIVED **Late Triassic-Early Jurassic 225–190 million years ago**

Plateosaurus was one of a group of very large plant-eating dinosaurs – the prosauropods. It grew to about 9 m (30 ft) long and was 3–4 m (10–13 ft) tall. It had strong limbs and a tail which made up almost half of its length. Its skull was small, with a snout which was quite narrow but strongly built and deeper than that of most other prosauropods. The upper and lower jaws held many serrated (saw-edged), leaf-shaped teeth.

Scientists are still debating how *Plateosaurus* looked, walked and fed. Perhaps, like severalprosauropods, it had a long-clawed 'thumb' (first digit) on its 'hands'. Some palaeontolgists believe that *Plateosaurus* walked on its hind legs. Others think that the huge claw was turned inwards and would hardly have touched the ground when the animal walked on all fours.

Perhaps in its search for food, *Plateosaurus* sometimes walked on two legs and sometimes on four.

About a hundred specimens of *Plateosaurus* have been found in Europe. It may be that the prosauropods roamed the world in small herds, feeding on the palm-like cycads and conifers.

Prosauropods

Mussasaurus muss-ah-saw-rus

Mouse Lizard

Saurischia • Sauropodomorpha • Prosauropoda • Family: Plateosauridae

FIRST DISCOVERED c.1978 • FOUND South America: Patagonia • LENGTH c.20 cm (8 in) • WEIGHT 2–3 kg (5–7 lb) • FOOD Plants • YOUNG Eggs • LIVED Late Triassic 216–203 million years ago

When it was discovered in the late 1970s, the tiny skeleton of *Mussasaurus* created a surge of interest in young (juvenile) dinosaurs. Several newly hatched animals and two small eggs of *Mussasaurus* were found in a 'nest site' in the Santa Cruz region of Patagonia in southern Argentina. The juvenile dinosaurs had obviously died soon after hatching. Their skulls were only 3–4 cm (1½ in) long but their eye sockets were very large, which is typical of most young reptiles.

Reconstructions of *Mussasaurus* show the animal as a tiny, long-necked, thin-legged creature with a head which was quite large and deep compared to its body. Both hands and feet were thought to have medium to long fingers and toes. Recently, palaeontogists have compared the skull and jaws of *Mussasaurus* with those of the much bigger *Coloradisaurus*, a

prosauropod dinosaur from southern Argentina. It is thought that adult *Coloradisaurus* grew to around 3–4 m (10–13 ft) long and weighed in at about 200–250 kg (450–550 lb) – a hundred times heavier than the *Mussasaurus*!

Prosauropods

Riojasaurus ree-o-ha-saw-rus

Rioja Lizard

Saurischia • Sauropodomorpha • Prosauropoda • Family: Uncertain

FIRST DISCOVERED 1967 • FOUND South America: Argentina • LENGTH c.6–10 m (20-33 ft) • WEIGHT 1–3 t •
FOOD Plants • YOUNG Eggs • LIVED Late Triassic 225–200 million years ago

Near the city of Rioja in Argentina, more than 20 skeletons of *Riojasaurus*, including adults and young animals, were found in Late Triassic rocks. *Riojasaurus* was a heavily built dinosaur with enormously powerful limbs. Its hind legs were slightly longer than the front limbs but it probably walked on all fours. It had a long neck and tail but a comparatively small, elongated head. The vertebrae (individual bones that make up the spine) were hollow.

Riojasaurus's teeth were leaf shaped and serrated (saw-edged). The upper jaw contained five teeth at the front, with 24 more behind them which extended a long way back into its skull. Many scientists think that *Riojasaurus* was closely related to *Melanosaurus*, the largest prosauropod known from the Triassic-Early Jurassic era. However, recent studies at Bristol University, England, suggest that it is unique in some key ways, such as the longer bones in its neck. It is certainly quite different from other prosauropods found in the Los Colarados Formation of Argentina.

Thecodontosaurus theek-oh-don-toe-saw-rus

Socket-toothed Lizard

Saurischia • Sauropodomorpha • Prosauropoda • Family: Thecodontosauridae

FIRST DISCOVERED • **1834** • FOUND **Europe: England, Wales** • LENGTH *c*.**2.5 m (8 ft)** • WEIGHT **4 t**
• FOOD **Plants** • YOUNG **Eggs** • LIVED **Late Triassic: 228–200 million years ago**

Interestingly, the first fossil remains of this ancient reptile were discovered well before Sir Richard Owen gave his famous talk on dinosaurs in 1841. Those early remains were found in the Clifton area of Bristol in the southwest of England, and *Thecodontosaurus* became the fourth type of dinosaur to be found in the United Kingdom.

Thecodontosaurus was a small to medium-sized prosauropod which probably ran on two legs. Although we do not have a complete picture of what the animal's skeleton looked like, the discovery of a young specimen in Wales has enabled us to reconstruct the overall form of *Thecodontosaurus*. Male thecodontosaurs seem to have been more heavily built than the females, like the males of many modern mammals.

Thecodontosaurus had rather a short neck supporting a fairly large skull with quite big eyes. Its jaws contained many small to medium-sized, serrated, leaf-like teeth. This prosauropod's hands and feet each had five digits, and the hands were long and rather narrow with an extended claw on each. This dinosaur's front limbs were much shorter than the legs, and its tail was much longer than the head, neck and body put together.

Prosauropods

Vulcanodon vol-kan-oh-don

Volcano tooth

Saurischia • Sauropodomorpha • Sauropoda • Family: Vulcanodontidae

FIRST DESCRIBED 1972 • FOUND **Africa: Zimbabwe, ?Asia** • LENGTH c.6–8 m (20–26 ft) • WEIGHT **1–2 t** •
FOOD **Plants** • YOUNG **Eggs** • LIVED **Early Jurassic 200–196 million years ago**

Primitive Sauropods

Vulcanodon is a primitive sauropod dinosaur. It is often illustrated as a bulky creature with rather short front legs and short neck. Like the prosauropods, its thumb had a strong claw that was directed slightly outwards away from the body. Its hips, too, resembled those of *Plateosaurus* (see page 20) and its other prosauropod cousins.

Vulcanodon and other dinosaurs closely related to it lived in Africa and possibly Asia. They probably lived alongside larger, more advanced sauropods. The *Vulcanodon*'s name is the result of a mistake! No skull remains of the *Vulcanodon* have yet been found, and it seems likely that the small, serrated teeth that were dug up with its incomplete skeleton in an area of volcanic rocks are, in fact, those of a small meat eater. So it shouldn't have been given the name 'Volcano Tooth' after all. Primitive sauropods spread quickly across the Late Triassic–Early Jurassic world.

Barapasaurus bah-rap-ah-saw-rus

Big Leg Lizard

Saurischia • Sauropodomorpha • Eusauropoda • Family: Barapasauridae

FIRST DISCOVERED 1960 • FOUND Asia: India • LENGTH c.14–18 m (46–60 ft) • WEIGHT 10-40 t • FOOD Plants
• YOUNG Eggs • LIVED Early Jurassic 183–176 million years ago

Like early prosauropods, the primitive sauropod dinosaur *Barapasaurus* has leaf-shaped, serrated teeth and, despite its name, quite slender limbs. More than 300 bones have been found and, together, they make up six incomplete skeletons. None of the skeletons has a skull or front or back feet. All the bones were discovered in the Early Jurassic rocks of the Godavari Valley in the Kota Region of southern India.

Compared with even the largest of the prosauropods, *Barapasaurus* was gigantic. Like most sauropods, it had a very long tail and a long neck probably supporting a small head. The individual bones that made up its spine had indentations in them, unlike the large hollows typical of more advanced sauropods such as *Brachiosaurus*. It is thought that these hollowed-out bones made the whole skeleton lighter – useful for such huge animals. No one is sure how heavy *Barapasaurus* was, though, and estimates vary wildly from person to person. It lived on coastal flood plains or deltas, and fed on plants.

Primitive Sauropods

Apatosaurus a-pat-oh-saw-rus

Deceptive Lizard

Saurischia • Sauropodomorpha • Sauropoda • Neosauropoda • Family: Diplodocidae

FIRST DESCRIBED 1877 • FOUND **North America** • LENGTH *c.*22–23 m (72–75 ft) • WEIGHT 25–30 t • FOOD Plants • YOUNG Eggs • LIVED Late Jurassic 161–145 million years ago

Sauropods

There are several different types of *Apatosaurus* known from Wyoming, Colorado, Oklahoma and Utah in the United States. When this giant sauropod was first identified and described, mistakes were made and the name *Brontosaurus* ('Thunder Reptile') was used for identical skeletal remains. For many years *Brontosaurus* was the more commonly used name.

Apatosaurus and *Diplodocus* (see page 27) both belong to the same family of sauropod dinosaurs, the Diplodocidae. *Diplodocus* was the longer of the two dinosaurs but *Apatosaurus* was much heavier. No skull of *Apatosaurus* has ever been found but it was probably similar to that of *Diplodocus*. *Apatosaurus* had a small brain. It relied heavily on its size for defence but there were two low ridges along its backbone which suggest that bundles of strong tendons (fibres which connect muscle to bone) or ligaments (fibres which connect bone to bone) held the neck high and enabled the animal to use its long tail like a mighty whip. The neck was about 6 m (20 ft) long and the tail was just over 9 m (30 ft). *Apatosaurus*'s legs were powerfully made and the back ones were longer than the front. Fossilized tracks have been found which indicate that *Apatosaurus* and *Diplodocus* swam in shallow water, using their front legs to push themselves forward.

Diplodocus dip-lod-oh-kus

Double-beam Lizard

Saurischia • Sauropodomorpha • Sauropoda • Neosauropoda • Family: Diplodocidae

FIRST DESCRIBED 1993 • FOUND **North America: USA** • LENGTH *c.*27 m (90 ft) • WEIGHT **10–25 t** • FOOD **Plants** • YOUNG **Eggs** • LIVED **Late Jurassic 161–146 million years ago**

Diplodocus and close relatives such as *Apatosaurus* (see page 26) and *Barosaurus* were the dominant plant eaters among the Late Jurassic dinosaur communities of North America. Five almost complete skeletons of *Diplodocus* have been found in the United States from Colorado, Utah, Wyoming and Montana. At the end of the 19th century hundreds of crates containing bones of the 'Double-beam Lizard' were sent back to the Carnegie Museum in Pittsburgh, Pennsylvania. You can see beautiful replicas of the complete skeleton in major museums through-out the world.

Diplodocus was a very long, quite slim sauropod. It had a remarkably long neck and a long, slender, whip-like tail. It stood tall, on long front legs, and it could stretch its long, horse-like head up to reach 10–12 m (30–40 ft) above the ground in search of soft vegetation from the treetops. The peg-like teeth occur only in the front of the mouth. Surprisingly, compared with giant sauropods such as *Argentinosaurus* (see page 31), *Diplodocus* was a lightweight. Huge tendons attached to its backbone enabled *Diplodocus* to hold both its neck and its tail high off the ground.

Sauropods

Seismosaurus size-moh-saw-rus
Earth-shaker Lizard

Saurischia • Sauropodomorpha • Sauropoda • Neosauropoda • Family: Diplodocidae

FIRST DESCRIBED 1991 • FOUND **North America: USA** • LENGTH *c.*40–50 m (130–165 ft) • WEIGHT **30–40 t**
• FOOD **Plants** • YOUNG **Eggs** • LIVED **Late Jurassic 145–161 million years ago**

Sauropods

There is no doubt that *Seismosaurus* was one of the biggest dinosaurs ever to walk on Earth. *Argentinosaurus* (see page 31) and *Supersaurus* are probably the main challengers for the title 'King of the Sauropods'.

In 1991 fossils from a huge new dinosaur were found. They included several backbones, part of a pelvis, some ribs and a number of V- or Y-shaped bones (chevrons) that are normally found on the lower side of the bones that make up the tail. From these bones a full-scale model of *Seismosaurus* was displayed at *Dinofest 2000* in Chicago. The missing bones were replaced by copies of bones from its close relatives scaled up to fit a *Seismosaurus*.

Not everybody believes that *Seismosaurus* existed. Recently some scientists have argued that the first description of it was wrong and that the remains are those of a new species of *Diplodocus* (see page 27).

Amargasaurus a-mar-gah-saw-rus

La Amarga Lizard

Saurischia • Sauropodomorpha • Sauropoda • Neosauropoda • Family: Dicraeosauridae

FIRST DESCRIBED **1991** • FOUND **South America: Argentina** • LENGTH **c.10 m (33 ft)** • WEIGHT **8–10 t**
• FOOD **Plants** • YOUNG **Eggs** • LIVED **Early Cretaceous 136–130 million years ago**

Amargasaurus was a medium-sized sauropod that lived in the La Amarga region of Argentina during the Early Cretaceous. It is unusual, however, in that its neck was short but had double row of tall spines. The spines were around 50 cm (1 ft 8 in) high and continued down its back. Some people believe that they supported a prominent, fleshy sail. Others think that dominant males had the biggest spines and that they were used in mating displays.

Amargasaurus, like other species of sauropod, was a plant eater, and its skull and teeth were similar to those of *Diplodocus* (see page 27). It had longer front legs so that the body sloped backwards towards the tail. All four feet resembled those of an elephant. Each foot had five toes and there was a claw on each inner toe. *Amargasaurus* probably lived in herds and ate conifers, cycads and seed ferns.

Sauropods

Brachiosaurus brack-ee-oh-saw-rus
Arm Lizard

Saurischia • Sauropodomorpha • Sauropoda • Macronaria • Family: Dicraeosauridae

FIRST DISCOVERED **1900** • FOUND **Africa; North America** • LENGTH **c.25 m (80 ft)** • WEIGHT **70–80 t**
• FOOD **Plants** • YOUNG **Eggs** • LIVED **Late Jurassic 161–146 million years ago**

Sauropods

Brachiosaurus has been found in Tanzania, East Africa, and Colorado in the United States. This shows us that in Late Jurassic times the two continents were one. *Brachiosaurus* was a gigantic creature with very long front limbs and shorter back limbs. It stood 16 m (over 50 ft) high and its weight was between 70 and 80 tonnes (as heavy as 18 to 20 elephants). The upper arm bone (humerus) was over 2 m (6½ ft) long.

Unlike those of *Diplodocus* (see page 27), the sturdy, chisel-like teeth of *Brachiosaurus* were arranged around the edges of the jawbones. This huge animal fed on leaves and shoots from the highest branches of trees, helped by its upward-sloping body. Its skull was about 50 cm (20 in) long

and much deeper than that of *Diplodocus*, and its nostrils opened at the top of the head. *Brachiosaurus's* neck was made up of 14 very large bones (vertebrae), and there were massive tendons to enable the animal to keep its head held high. Tendons and ligaments would also have helped hold the tail straight. A lash of that great tail would have deterred most predators.

Argentinosaurus ahr-gent-teen-oh-saw-rus

Argentina Lizard

Saurischia • Sauropodomorpha • Sauropoda • Neosauropoda • Macronaria
• Family: Andesauridae

FIRST DESCRIBED **1993** • FOUND **South America: Argentina** • LENGTH **c.40–41 m (131–135 ft)** • WEIGHT **80–90 t**
• FOOD **Plants** • YOUNG **Eggs** • LIVED **Middle–Upper Cretaceous 100–93 million years ago**

Argentinosaurus must have been a truly enormous creature – among the most gigantic animals ever to walk on Earth. Sadly, so far it is known only from a few leg bones, pieces of hip and some super-size back bones, several of which are more than 1 m (about 4 ft) long.

Reconstructed models suggest that *Argentinosaurus* was a typical sauropod with a small head, a long neck and a long tail. Closely related dinosaurs feature a sloping head, peg-like teeth and front limbs shorter than back ones. These creatures belong to a family of large sauropods from South America and possibly Africa. The forelimbs are longer than those of *Diplodocus* (see page 27) and the head is rather squarer in shape.

Sauropods

Saltasaurus salt-ah-saw-rus
Salta Lizard

Saurischia • Sauropodomorpha • Sauropoda • Titanosauria • Family: Saltasauridae

FIRST DISCOVERED ?1929 • FOUND South America: Argentina • LENGTH c.12–13 m (39–43 ft) • WEIGHT 10 t
• FOOD Plants • YOUNG Eggs • LIVED Late Cretaceous 83–70 million years ago

Saltasaurus is an interesting creature. At first it was just described as an armoured dinosaur, but in 1980 scientists recognized that it was a unique kind of sauropod. People became confused because patches of a bony 'coat' – made up of small, rounded and tightly packed 'scales' and larger plate-like bones – had been found with the original pieces of fossilized skeleton. *Saltasaurus* was an armoured sauropod. The bones were formed in the skin of the animal and would have given it some protection against its enemies. *Saltasaurus* existed in the Salta Region of Argentina during the Late Cretaceous.

Saltasaurus was a medium-sized sauropod with a relatively short neck but long, whip-like tail. The front and back legs were the same length and it walked on all fours. Eggs and embryos have been found which scientists think belong to *Saltasaurus*. These suggest that the bony scales appeared after hatching and that the teeth were long and sometimes chisel-like. The shells of *Saltasaurus* eggs were an amazing 15 cm (6 in) thick.

Sauropods

Camarasaurus kam-ah-rah-saw-rus

Chambered Lizard

Saurischia • Sauropodomorpha • Sauropoda • Macronaria • Family: Camarasauridae

FIRST DISCOVERED 1877 • FOUND **North America: USA; ?Europe** • LENGTH *c.*18 m (60 ft) • WEIGHT 25–30 t • FOOD **Plants** • YOUNG **Eggs** • LIVED **Late Jurassic 161–146 million years ago**

Although the first fossilized bones of *Camarasaurus* were found as early as 1877, scientists had to wait until 1925 for the first complete skeleton to be discovered. *Camarasaurus* has been found in Late Jurassic rocks in Colorado, New Mexico, Wyoming, Utah and Montana, in the United States. Bones have also been found in southern England that may belong to it. *Camarasaurus* was very common in North America in the Late Jurassic.

Most sauropods were herd-dwellers and *Camarasaurus* was probably no exception. Just as with today's animals of the great African savannas, it was important for the different species to be able to recognize one another. Although *Camarasaurus* was relatively small compared to other sauropods, its box-like snout and robust, chisel-like teeth gave it a distinctive look. It had a lightly built skull and there were large holes for the nostrils in front of the eye sockets. It had a heavily built body and a comparatively short tail.

It is thought that, like elephants, *Camarasaurus* had wedge-like heels of soft tissue on its feet to help support its weight.

Sauropods

Haplocanthosaurus hap-loh-kan-thoh-saw-rus

Single-spine Lizard

Saurischia • Sauropodomorpha • Sauropoda • Macronaria • Family: Haplocanthosauridae

FIRST DESCRIBED 1903 • FOUND **North America: USA; ?Africa** • LENGTH *c.*22 m (72 ft) • WEIGHT 20 t • FOOD **Plants** • YOUNG **Eggs** • LIVED Late Jurassic 156–151 million years ago

Sauropods

Haplocanthosaurus was originally known as *Morosaurus agilis*. Scientists are still unsure about the remains that have been found of this Late Jurassic sauropod, mainly because it shares the characteristics of animals from several families. The shape and structure of the bones of the spine between the neck and the hips are the cause of much argument.

Haplocanthosaurus has been found in Colorado and Wyoming in the United States. The most complete example is in the Kirtland Gallery of the Cleveland Museum of Natural History, Ohio. This individual is known locally as 'Happy', but the species is named *H. delfsi* after Edwin R. Delfs. In 1954, as a young man of 20, Delfs led an expedition of four friends into the wilds of Colorado. They found the bones of 'Happy' and now, 50 years later, after a career in medicine, Delfs has come back to hunting for dinosaurs. 'Happy' has a horse-like head, chisel-like teeth and large, padded feet.

Mamenchisaurus mah-men-kee-saw-rus

Mamenxi (Ferry) Lizard

Saurischia • Sauropodomorpha • Sauropoda • Macronaria • Family: Euhelopodidae

FIRST DESCRIBED 1954 • FOUND Asia: China • LENGTH *c.*25 m (82 ft) • WEIGHT 18–20 t • FOOD Plants
• YOUNG Eggs • LIVED Late Jurassic 151-146 million years ago

Mamenchisaurus has one of the biggest necks of all the sauropod dinosaurs, with 19 long neck bones. Some individuals may even have had necks more than 15 m (49 ft) long, almost half the total length of the animal. Reconstructions make it look as if it was rather a slow, awkward mover. Long, bony struts lessened sideways movement in the neck. It seems likely that *Mamenchisaurus* spent much of its life feeding from the treetops.

Four species of the 'Mamenxi Lizard' have been found in Late Jurassic rocks of the Szechuan, Ganzu and Xinjiang provinces of China. The fossils were discovered in rocks laid down in fresh water where there may have been a monsoon climate (with seasonal strong winds and hard rain). There are few skulls but, from what we have, the animal seems to have had a blunt snout and spatula-shaped teeth. At first, people thought that *Mamenchisaurus* was related to the American diplodocids but recent tests suggest that it belongs to a group of sauropods so far found only in Asia.

Sauropods

Nemegtosaurus nem-egg-toe-saw-rus

Nemegt Lizard

Saurischia • Sauropodomorpha • Sauropoda • Neosauropoda • Family: Nemegtosauridae

FIRST DESCRIBED 1971 • FOUND Asia: Mongolia • LENGTH c.25 m (82 ft) • WEIGHT 18–20 t • FOOD Plants
• YOUNG Eggs • LIVED Late Cretaceous 71–66 million years ago

Known only from a single skull, *Nemegtosaurus* is a hard nut to crack. Scientists are not sure which dinosaurs it is most closely related to. Recently, they have suggested that it may be related to the titanosaurs. In fact, *Nemegtosaurus* and *Quaesitosaurus*, also from Mongolia, may be the same animal. If they are, this would mean

that the group survived from Late Jurassic times through to the Late Cretaceous – a span of almost 90 million years.

The remains of another Late Cretaceous sauropod from Mongolia, *Opisthocoelicaudia*, have also been associated with *Nemegtosaurus*, but sadly these remains do not include the

skull or the neck. The bulky body, sturdy legs and short, strong tail, held high off the ground resemble those of *Nemegtosaurus*'s family. Perhaps *Opisthocoelicaudia* used its tail and hind legs as a steadying 'tripod' when it was feeding. Skull material from *Phuwiangosaurus* may help with our knowledge of this family.

Herrerasaurus her-rare-ah-saw-rus

Herrera's Lizard

Saurischia • Theropoda • Family: Herrerasauridae

First Discovered **1963** • Found **South America: Argentina** • Length **c.2.5 m (8 ft)** • Weight **30 kg (66 lb)**
• Food **Meat** • Young **Eggs** • Lived **Late Triassic 228–200 million years ago**

The first bones of *Herrerasaurus* were discovered in 1963 but the first scientific description was not made until 1988. Together with *Caseosaurus*, *Chindesaurus* and *Staurikosaurus*, it makes up a group of primitive theropod dinosaurs found only in South America. This animal is named after the Argentine farmer who first found it, Victorino Herrera.

Herrerasaurus had a long, lizard-like head armed with many serrated, conical teeth. It was lightly built, with hollow, thin-walled bones. It walked or ran on its two long hind legs and it also had a long, whip-like tail. It had quite short arms and the first finger of each hand was made up of just a

single bone. As with other agile, fast-moving theropods, *Herrerasaurus* could grip its prey tightly between its fingers and thumb. Rather like some modern snakes, it had loosely jointed jaws that could open wide so that it could eat large prey.

Theropods

Eoraptor ee-oh-rap-tor

Dawn Plunderer

Saurischia • Theropoda • Family: Eoraptidae

FIRST DISCOVERED **1991** • FOUND **South America: Argentina** • LENGTH *c.*1 m (3 ft 3 in) • WEIGHT **9 kg (20 lb)** • FOOD **Meat** • YOUNG **Eggs** • LIVED **Late Triassic 228–200 million years ago**

Theropods

Eoraptor and *Herrerasaurus* (see page 37) lived in the same area of Argentina at the same time. They were both primitive theropods. *Eoraptor* was about a third of the size of its larger cousin. It was very lightly built, with a narrow skull in which there were many small, saw-edged teeth. It had long hind legs which it ran on to pursue its prey. The arms were short, with five fingers on each hand, although the fourth and fifth were quite short. Like *Herrerasaurus*, *Eoraptor* could hold its food firmly

as the thumb could turn slightly over the palm of the hand. This is called an 'opposable' thumb. Humans and the great apes also have this kind of thumb.

Although *Eoraptor* and *Herrerasaurus* share many characteristics, their teeth and fingers are different. As well as being smaller, *Eoraptor* is the more primitive of the two and is closer to the earliest stage of

dinosaur evolution than most other animals that lived at the same time. Among theropod dinosaurs, having five complete fingers is a primitive state. *Herrerasaurus* effectively has four, *Coelophysis* (see page 39) three and *Tyrannosaurus* (see page 64) just two.

Coelophysis see-loh-fy-sis

Hollow Form

Saurischia • Theropoda • Neotheropoda • Family: Coelophysidae

FIRST DESCRIBED **1881** • FOUND **North America: United States** • LENGTH **c.3 m (10 ft)** • WEIGHT **20–30 kg (44-66 lb)** • FOOD **Meat** • YOUNG **Eggs** • LIVED **Late Triassic 228–200 million years ago**

The name 'Hollow Form' aptly describes this small, hollow-boned theropod dinosaur. Known initially from a few bones found in Arizona, *Coelophysis* attained great fame in 1947, when the renowned American palaeontologist Edwin Colbert (1905–2001) discovered about a hundred skeletons at the Ghost Ranch in New Mexico. From the skeletons, it seems that the animals may have drowned during a flash flood, when torrents of floodwater, mud and boulders thundered down the valley after very heavy rain.

This dramatic find showed that large numbers of these small, meat-eating, scavenging dinosaurs lived in the same area and that the population included males and females. The skeletons of young animals were found inside some adults, so could *Coelophysis* have given birth to live young or could it have been a cannibal? All dinosaurs laid eggs so *Coelophysis* must have eaten its own kind! Four long fingers and four long toes show that *Coelophysis* was more advanced than either *Eoraptor* (see page 38) or *Herrerasaurus* (see page 37). The fourth finger was also shortened, so it seems that *Coelophysis* had advanced one stage closer to having three-digit limbs.

Theropods

Podokesaurus poh-doke-ee-saw-rus

Swift-footed Lizard

Saurischia • Theropoda • Neotheropoda • Family: Coelophysidae

FIRST DESCRIBED 1911 • FOUND **North America: USA** • LENGTH **c.90 cm (3 ft)** • WEIGHT **3–6 kg (6.6–13 lb)** • FOOD **Meat** • YOUNG **Eggs** • LIVED **Early Jurassic 200–183 million years ago**

Theropods

Unfortunately, the fossil remains of this small, swift-running dinosaur were destroyed by fire. Luckily, however, the original bones had been copied as casts. *Podokesaurus* is still a problem, though: many scientists believe that the bones are actually those of a young *Coelophysis* (see page 39). If this is true, then *Coelophysis* would have lived on Earth for approximately 45 million years! This would place it among the most successful dinosaurs of all time. Perhaps its ability to survive on a wide variety of food, including small reptiles, crayfish, freshwater clams and even the young of its own kind, was the secret of its success.

Little or no skull material has been found but the limb and hip bones indicate that *Podokesaurus* was very lightly built and only 30 cm (1 ft) tall. Like the many skeletons of *Coelophysis* from New Mexico, the original *Podokesaurus* fossils, and the boulder they were in, were plucked from their original burial site and carried by a glacier (a huge river of ice) to Holyoke, Massachusetts during the last Ice Age.

Dilophosaurus di-loaf-oh-saw-rus

Double-crested Lizard

Saurischia • Theropoda • Neotheropoda • Coelophysoidea • Family: Dilophosauridae

FIRST DISCOVERED **1942** • FOUND **North America: USA; China** • LENGTH **c.6 m (20 ft)**
• WEIGHT **450 kg (990 lb)** • FOOD **Meat** • YOUNG **Eggs** • LIVED **Early Jurassic 200–183 million years ago**

Dilophosaurus stood 3 m (10 ft) tall and had two crests or ridges on the top of its head. These crests stretched from just over the nostrils to the back of the skull. Its jaws were armed with many long, sharp, slender teeth. The arms were strongly built and the hands had three long fingers, one of which was shortened, just like those of *Coelophysis* (see page 39). All the indications are that this dinosaur was a medium-sized killer. *Dilophosaurus* probably used its arms and legs in the trapping and killing of its prey.

In the 1993 film, *Jurassic Park*, *Dilophosaurus* appeared as a poison-spitting meat eater which made use of its extended neck frill to startle its prey. Some birds and lizards can display their feathers or scaly frills to frighten away an attacker or during mating, but no bird or lizard is known to spit poison. *Dilophosaurus* may have had air sacs connected with the twin crests and could, perhaps, have inflated these either as a display to other males or as a way of being recognized.

Theropods

Gasosaurus gaz-oh-saw-rus

Gas Lizard

Saurischia • Theropoda • Neotheropoda • ?Tetanurae • Family: uncertain
FIRST DESCRIBED 1985 • FOUND Asia: China • LENGTH *c.*4 m (13 ft) • WEIGHT 150 kg (330 lb) • FOOD Meat
•YOUNG Eggs • LIVED Late Jurassic 161-146 million years ago

Theropods

The remains of *Gasosaurus* were discovered by the Chinese expert, Professor Dong Zhiming (1937–), who is often described as the 'world's greatest dinosaur hunter'. Professor Dong has found over a hundred dinosaur skeletons. His first finds were in 1963. He has devoted his life to studying fossilized backboned animals (vertebrate palaeontology), and seems to enjoy naming the dinosaurs he often unearths in his beloved country.

The full name of this medium-sized meat eater is *Gasosaurus constructus* because it was found on the gas and oil company construction site in Dashanpu. There is not enough material to place the 'Gas Lizard' in a particular family.

No skull fragments have been found up to now of *Gasosaurus* . It is usually illustrated, however, as a very fierce-looking theropod that attacked its prey in small groups. It is supposed to have had a large head and many sharp, saw-edged teeth. None of this can be confirmed at the present time, but it does show that, for dinosaurs at least, art sometimes overtakes science.

Ceratosaurus ser-ah-toe-saw-rus

Horned Lizard

Saurischia • Theropoda • Neotheropoda • Family: Ceratosauridae

FIRST DESCRIBED **1884** • FOUND **North America: USA; Africa** • LENGTH **c.6 m (20 ft)** • WEIGHT **1 t**
• FOOD **Meat** • YOUNG **Eggs** • LIVED **Late Jurassic–Early Cretaceous 161–140 million years ago**

Ceratosaurus was a medium-sized theropod with a large head sporting a horn above the nose. It also had massive dagger-like teeth. It was first found in the western part of North America and lived at the same time as *Allosaurus* (see page 53). In fact, the bones of both dinosaurs have been found in the same quarry!

Described by the American palaeontologist, Othniel C. Marsh (1832–99), in 1884, *Ceratosaurus* was at first thought to have been a good swimmer, and to have used its long, thin tail to propel it through the water. This is extremely unlikely, however, as Ceratosaurus was quite heavily built and had short arms and powerful legs. It was, in fact, a fast runner and caught and killed its prey by crushing them in its massive, strong jaws. In comparison with *Allosaurus*, *Ceratosaurus* was a small but well-equipped rival.

Ceratosaurus had a horn on its nose. It also had two smaller horns over its eyebrows and some people think that together these provided protection in battle. Others think that the nasal horn was for display in dominant males. *Ceratosaurus* has been found in Utah and Colorado in the United States and Tanzania in East Africa.

Theropods

Majungalothus ma-jung-ga-loth-us

Majunga Dome Lizard

Saurischia • Theropoda • Neotheropoda • Family: Abelisauridae

FIRST DISCOVERED **1974** • FOUND **Africa: Madagascar** • LENGTH *c.*10 m (33 ft) • WEIGHT **4–5 t** • FOOD **Meat**
• YOUNG **Eggs** • LIVED **Late Cretaceous 83–71 million years ago**

Theropods

Majungalothus is a short-faced, dome-headed theropod. It was first discovered in 1974 in the Majunga Province of northern Madagascar. In 1998, two beautifully preserved specimens, including an almost complete skull, were found. The skull was characteristically 'domed', with large eye sockets behind two rather small, rounded openings for the nostrils. The powerful jaws were wide and armed with robust, saw-edged teeth. *Majungalothus* was a meat eater.

Normally we might have expected to find that this big theropod hunted the giant sauropods that lived in the swamplands of Majunga Province. However, recent studies have shown that some *Majungalothus* bones bear dinosaur tooth marks which turn out to be those of another *Majungalothus*. Cannibalism, among dinosaurs at least, seems to have been common during the Late Cretaceous in Madagascar. We could say that the food chain started at home!

Carnotaurus car-noh-tor-us

Flesh Bull

Saurischia • Theropoda • Neotheropoda • Family: Abelisauridae

FIRST DISCOVERED **1985** • FOUND **South America: Patagonia** • LENGTH **c.9 m (30 ft)** • WEIGHT **3–4 t**
• FOOD **Meat** • YOUNG **Eggs** • LIVED **Middle Cretaceous 83–71 million years ago**

Carnotaurus and *Carnotosaurus* are the alternative names given to a large-headed, medium- to large-sized meat eater from the Middle Cretaceous of Patagonia in southern Argentina. Not only was its head big, it was also deep and had a short, bulldog-like face. Both names suggest that this was a bull-like dinosaur that ate meat. *Carnotaurus* had rather thin jawbones but the teeth were strong and saw-edged. They tended to splay outwards from the jaws, giving the face an even stranger appearance. The animal walked on its hind legs and probably had little or no use for its arms because they were ridiculously short and had only two fingers that actually functioned.

When *Carnotaurus* was first discovered, there were detailed impressions of a scaly skin on the right side of the body. The scales do not appear to have overlapped and most are raised as small to medium-sized, knobby swellings.

Theropods

Abelisaurus ah-bell-ee-sawr-us

Abel's Lizard

Saurischia • Theropoda • Neotheropoda • Family: Abelisauridae

FIRST DISCOVERED **1985** • FOUND **South America** • LENGTH **c.7 m (23 ft)** • WEIGHT **1.5 t** • FOOD **Meat**
• YOUNG **Eggs** • LIVED **Late Cretaceous 75–70 million years ago**

Theropods

Abelisaurus is a meat eater known from just a single skull found in the Rio Negro Province of Argentina, and was first described in 1985. The skull is quite high and large at 85 cm (33 inches) with a rounded snout and many small, saw-edged teeth. Although the head of *Abelisaurus* is broad, the face is relatively short. An unusual feature of this theropod is a large opening on the side of the skull in front of the eye sockets.

The abelisaur dinosaurs are two-legged hunters that grew to 9 m (30 ft) in length. Representatives of the family are found in Africa, Asia and South America. *Carnotaurus* (see page 45) and *Majungatholus* (see page 44) are members of the *Abelisaurdae*. Some of these animals have distinctive horns or dome-like growths on their skulls. Most have large eyes and short arms. *Abelisaurus* is usually illustrated as a small, rather fat-necked Tyrannosaurus-like dinosaur (see page 64). Most people who study dinosaurs, however, suggest that they are placed on separate branches of the dinosaur evolutionary tree.

Baryonyx bar-ee-on-ix

Heavy Claw

Saurischia • Theropoda • Tetanurae • Family: Spinosauridae

FIRST DISCOVERED **1983** • FOUND **Europe: England; Africa** • LENGTH **c.9.5 m (31 ft)** • WEIGHT **1.5–2 t**
• FOOD **Fish, carrion** • YOUNG **Eggs** • LIVED **Early–Middle Cretaceous 125–94 million years ago**

Baryonyx was discovered in a clay pit in Surrey, southeast England, in 1983 by William Walker. It gets its name because of the fearsome-looking, 30-cm-long (1 ft), curved claw on the inside of each hand.

It lived in a subtropical, marshy or swampy environment alongside the plant eater *Iguanodon* (see page 106) and had a rather flattened skull, a long snout and small, saw-edged teeth. The front limbs were comparatively short but very powerful, with strong, grasping hands. The huge claw was probably used to slash at the entrails of dead animals and as a 'hook' with which to hold or even catch fish. The stomach remains of *Baryonyx* show that fish and perhaps even *Iguanodon* were part of its last meal. The crocodile-like snout and the strong hands suggest that *Baryonyx* fished in much the same way as a modern brown bear catches salmon.

Theropods

Irritator ir-ee-tay-tor

Irritation

Saurischia • Theropoda • Avetheropoda • Family: Spinosauridae

FIRST DESCRIBED **1996** • FOUND **South America: Brazil** • LENGTH **c.8 m (26 ft)** • WEIGHT **1–1.5 t** • FOOD **Meat** • YOUNG **Eggs** • LIVED **Early Cretaceous 125–100 million years ago**

Irritator could be defined as the 'one who likes to irritate'. The name was chosen by the scientists who first described this large Brazilian meat eater to register their anger at the modification of the skull by local 'craftsmen'. Many wonderful fossils have been found in the Santana Formation of the Chapada do Aripe area of north-eastern Brazil. They are a source of income for many local people, who often work on their finds in order to make them more attractive and increase sales. Beautiful fish remains, as well as turtles and pterosaurs, proclaim the importance of this very special site.

The skull remains of *Irritator* are kept in the Natural History Museum in Stuttgart, Germany, and it is possible that a passing scientist bought them rather than finding them. The remains are similar to the skulls of *Baryonyx* (see page 47) and *Spinosaurus* (see page 49) although *Irritator* carried a crest. There may have been muscles attached to the crest or it may have been a display feature of a dominant male. Reconstructions of *Irritator* show that it had a large head and that the three-fingered hands bore claws and were very powerful.

Spinosaurus spy-noh-saw-rus

Spiny Lizard

Saurischia • Theropoda • Avetheropoda • Family: Spinosauridae

FIRST DESCRIBED 1915 • FOUND Africa: Egypt, Tunisia, Morocco • LENGTH c.12 m (40 ft) • WEIGHT 6 t
• FOOD Meat • YOUNG Eggs • LIVED Early–Middle Cretaceous 135–90 million years ago

Some scientist say that *Spinosaurus* may have reached lengths of 15–16 m (49–52 ft), the skull alone being 2.4 m (8 ft) long. Normal specimens would have been about 12 m (40 ft) long and 5 m (16 ft) tall. Much of the original material collected was destroyed during a bombing raid on Munich during the Second World War in 1944. However, *Spinosaurus* is well known from sites in North Africa. Hundreds of teeth have been collected from Morocco and Tunisia.

The teeth are long and conical with a circular cross-section and have well-developed grooves running downwards from a pointed tip. The skull was long and flat, almost like a crocodile's. *Spinosaurus* probably fed mainly on fish. It was quite heavily built, with strong arms and three-clawed hands, but its most spectacular feature was its 'sail'. Blade-like spines 1.6 m (5 ft 2½ in) high along its back supported this fantastic flap. The spines would have been covered by skin and muscle. Arguments abound as to the function of the sail: some say it was part of a mating display; others that it acted like a radiator, helping the animal to warm up quickly.

Theropods

Eustreptospondylus you-strep-toe-spon-dye-lus
True Reversed Vertebrae

Saurischia • Theropoda • Tetanurae • Family: Eustreptospondylidae

FIRST DISCOVERED 1871 • FOUND Europe: England • LENGTH c.5 m (16 ft) • WEIGHT 800 kg (1,760 lb)
• FOOD Meat • YOUNG Eggs • LIVED Late Jurassic 160–155 million years ago

Theropods

This theropod is known from a single skeleton found in an Oxford clay quarry in Midlands Britain. The quarry is now covered by school playing fields. The Oxford clay was laid down in the sea, and the most common fossils in it are ammonites (spiral-shelled creatures), belemnites (creatures related to squid, octopus and cuttlefish which have bullet-shaped shells) and clams. These are hardly the creatures you would associate with a meat-eating dinosaur. *Eustreptospondylus* probably died while hunting on the banks of a river; it may have fallen in and was then carried out to sea. The skeleton is of a young animal and it is likely that adults were much larger. Typically, this dinosaur would probably have had a large head armed with sharp teeth, as well as short arms and a long tail. Some scientists think that *Eustreptospondylus* was a direct ancestor of certain giant theropods of the Late Cretaceous, including *Giganotosaurus* (see page 57).

Megalosaurus meg-al-oh-saw-rus

Big Lizard

Saurischia • Theropoda • Tetanurae • Family: Megalosauridae

FIRST DISCOVERED **1818** • FOUND **Europe: England, Wales, France; ?South America; ?Asia; ?Africa** • LENGTH **c.9 m (30 ft)** • WEIGHT **1.5 t** • FOOD **Meat** • YOUNG **Eggs** • LIVED **Middle Jurassic–Late Cretaceous 165–75 million years ago**

Megalosaurus is unique. It was the first dinosaur to be described; it was probably the first to be discovered, and it was one of the first to be modelled and shown to the public. The English clergyman-geologist, William Buckland (1784–1856) described *Megalosaurus* in 1824, from fossils discovered in 1818. The first evidence of this giant meat eater, however, was a large fragment of a thigh bone illustrated by the English naturalist, Robert Plot (1640–96), in 1677.

Over the last hundred years, other much larger meat-eating dinosaurs have been discovered, but none of these can take *Megalosaurus*'s place as the first of an amazing group of reptiles. Originally, *Megalosaurus* was found only in southern England, but a jawbone has since been discovered in South Wales, and other remnants in France and else-where have shown that the animal had an international presence.

Megalosaurus had three fingers on each hand and four toes on its feet. It had large, saw-edged teeth that curved slightly backwards. It was a very successful predator that roamed Earth for almost 100 hundred million years.

Theropods

Monolophosaurus mono-loaf-oh-saw-rus
Single-crested Lizard

Saurischia • Theropoda • Tetanurae • Carnosauria • Family: Allosauridae

FIRST DISCOVERED **1984** • FOUND **Asia: China** • LENGTH **c.6 m (20 ft)** • WEIGHT **700 kg (1,540 lb)** • FOOD **Meat** • YOUNG **Eggs** • LIVED **Middle Jurassic 175–162 million years ago**

Theropods

We are not sure about the true family links of this theropod dinosaur. Some scientists claim that it is a relative of *Megalosaurus* (see page 51), while others argue that it is closer to *Allosaurus* (see page 53). *Monolophosaurus* is characterized by a single, hollow crest on top of its head which connects with the nasal cavities. The crest may have been used in display but some people think that it acted as a 'sound box', enabling the animal to contact friends or frighten away enemies.

The head was large and narrow and the jaws held many sharp, slightly backward-curving teeth. Overall, *Monolophosaurus* was heavily built, with strong forelimbs. Each of its hands was armed with three powerful, long-clawed fingers. The hind limbs were also strongly built and it is likely that this formidable hunter could attack and kill quite large prey.

Monolophosaurus is known only from one incomplete skeleton, so it is impossible to say if it hunted in 'packs'. Some descriptions of the creature suggest that it might have spent part of its time in water, but this seems unlikely for such a big predator.

Allosaurus al-oh-saw-rus

Different Lizard

Saurischia • Theropoda • Tetanurae • Carnosauria • Family: Allosauridae

FIRST DISCOVERED **1869** • FOUND **North America: USA** • LENGTH **c.12 m (40 ft)** • WEIGHT **2–4 t** • FOOD **Meat** • YOUNG **Eggs** • LIVED **Late Jurassic 160–145 million years ago**

Since 1988, *Allosaurus* has been the state fossil of Utah in the United States. Indeed, it has become almost legendary because of the huge number of specimens discovered in two quarries in the centre of the state. Originally known from just a single section of tail from Colorado, *Allosaurus* is now represented by over 60 specimens, including males, females and young. Compared to *Tyrannosaurus* (see page 64), *Allosaurus*'s skull was lightly built and its teeth were relatively small. Even so, it has been worked out that it could still take 30-cm (1-ft) bites, and bite marks have been found on the tail section of an *Apatosaurus* (see page 26). It is unlikely that a single *Allosaurus* could bring down and kill this huge plant eater but a 'pack' of large adults certainly could.

Some people think that *Allosaurus* could run at speeds close to 40 mph (64 kph). Armed with its many sharp, saw-edged teeth and claws sometimes described as 'talon-like', a fast-moving *Allosaurus* would have been a formidable enemy.

Theropods

Yangchuanosaurus yang-shoo-an-oh-saw-rus

Yangchuan Lizard

Saurischia • Theropoda • Tetanurae • Carnosauria • Family: Sinraptoridae

FIRST DESCRIBED **1978** • FOUND **Asia: China** • LENGTH **c.9 m (29½ ft)** • WEIGHT **2–3 t** • FOOD **Meat** • YOUNG **Eggs** • LIVED **Late Jurassic 160–145 million years ago**

Yangchuanosaurus is a primitive relative of *Allosaurus* (see page 53). It is closely related to *Sinoraptor* and *Lourinhanosaurus*, two meat eaters from China and Portugal. Their distribution suggests that the family members evolved to occupy similar environments to those dominated by the allosaurids in North America. The 'Yangchuan Lizard' was found in the Sichuan Province of China.

The fossil remains are incomplete but, using several specimens, it is possible to build a model of this large meat eater. Its head was over 1 m (3 ft 2 in) long and may have had a crest and a bony knob over the snout. The backward-curving teeth were rather dagger-like. Overall, the skull was lightly built, with several large openings that would have lessened its weight so that the animal would have been more agile. The eyes faced slightly forward to improve its ability to judge distance. This was a distinct advantage for a meat eater. Huge clawed hands enabled *Yangchuanosaurus* to grip, tear and rip at its prey. The big head was balanced out with a long tail that was held high above the ground. Good balance and powerful hind limbs suggest that *Yangchuanosaurus* was a fast runner and deadly in attack.

Acrocanthosaurus ak-ro-kan-tho-saw-rus

High-spined Lizard

Saurischia • Theropoda • Tetanurae • Carnosauria • Family: Allosauridae

FIRST DESCRIBED **1950** • FOUND **North America: USA** • LENGTH **c.12 m (40 ft)** • WEIGHT **2–4 t** • FOOD **Meat** • YOUNG **Eggs** • LIVED **Early-Mid Cretaceous 125–112 million years ago**

Down in the bed of the Paluxy River, near Glen Rose in Texas in the United States, two sets of footprints show that *Acrocanthosaurus* was tracking its next meal. Its prey, according to the second set of prints, preserved in the fine sediments of the Glen Rose Formation, was a *Pleurocoelus*, a giant sauropod. The prints reveal something of the hunting habits of the giant meat eater. They also show that the sauropods had developed a defence strategy, with the largest animals on the outside of the herd – like a herd of buffalo in which the big bulls protect the cows and young from lions.

During Early to Mid Cretaceous times, in what is now the southwestern part of the United States, *Acrocanthosaurus* was close to being a top predator. It had huge teeth with long roots. The teeth were slightly curved but thin and, unlike those of *Tyrannosaurus* (see page 64), probably broke quite easily. The broken tooth was then shed and another one grew in its place. The meat eater had powerful arms with sharp claws. It was a perfectly balanced hunter, with a strong, muscular back, and it ran on its hind legs. The 60-cm high (2-ft) spines over the bones of the back would have supported huge muscles.

Theropods

Carcharodontosaurus car-sha-ro-dont-oh-saw-rus

Shark-toothed Lizard

Saurischia • Theropoda • Tetanurae • Carnosauria • Family: Carcharodontosauridae

FIRST DESCRIBED 1931 • FOUND **Africa: Morocco, Niger, Tunisia, Libya, Egypt** • LENGTH **c.14 m (46 ft)**
• WEIGHT **6–8 t** • FOOD **Meat** • YOUNG **Eggs** • LIVED **Mid–Late Cretaceous 112–96 million years ago**

Theropods

Fossil remains of *Carcharodonto-saurus* were first found in the early 1920s, but were wrongly thought to be from a *Megalosaurus* (see page 51). Then, in 1931, they were correctly identified and, in 1995, a complete skull from Morocco confirmed that *Carcharodontosaurus* was one of the largest meat-eating dinosaurs ever found. Based on the Moroccan skull, the head would have been over 1.5 m (5 ft) long. It was armed with huge, triangular-shaped, saw-edged teeth that were about 15 cm (6 in) long.

Apart from the skull, not much else from the skeleton of *Carcharo-dontosaurus* has been found, so we cannot be sure at the moment exactly what it looked like overall. It is a safe bet, however, to illustrate it as a gigantic two-legged meat eater with shortened arms and powerful three-fingered hands. The skull of *Carcharodontosaurus* appears to be slightly shorter than that of *Giganotosaurus* (see page 57), a close relative. Looking at the quite small braincases of both *Carcharodontosaurus* and *Tyrannosaurus rex* (see page 64), we might assume that the 'shark-toothed lizard' was a little lacking in brainpower!

Giganotosaurus ji-ga-note-oh-saw-rus

Giant Southern Lizard

Saurischia • Theropoda • Tetanurae • Carnosauria • Family: Carcharodontosauridae

FIRST DESCRIBED **1995** • FOUND **South America** • LENGTH **c.14 m (46 ft)** • WEIGHT **6–8 t** • FOOD **Meat**
• YOUNG **Eggs** • LIVED **Late Cretaceous 96 million years ago**

Giganotosaurus is a cousin of *Carcharodontosaurus* (see page 56) and both are close relatives of *Allosaurus* (see page 53). Even among these huge meat eaters,

however, *Giganotosaurus* stood out as a giant. Its skull was over 1.9 m (6 ft) long and the body was very heavily built, with three talon-like claws on each hand. Some scientists argue that it is the same genus as *Carcharodontosaurus*, suggesting that the South American animals were larger than their African relatives.

During the late 1990s several discoveries – including a number of *Giganotosaurus* skeletons – on the same site suggested that these giants hunted in 'packs'. A pack would have shadowed a large herd of sauropods for many miles and, as the great plant eaters began to tire, gaps in their defences would appear.

Older animals may have slowed down, so that the young at the centre of the herd were exposed. The relatively quick-footed predators may then have been able to single out smaller or weaker victims. Killing 100-tonne giant would be a challenge but a ten-tonne baby or an injured adult would have been easy prey. Once again, this is how a pride of lions or a pack of hyenas on the African plains might organize a hunting party.

Theropods

Compsognathus kom-sog-nay-thus
Pretty Jaw

Saurischia • Theropoda • Tetanurae • Coelurosauria • Family: Compsognathidae

FIRST DISCOVERED 1859 • FOUND Europe: France, Germany • LENGTH c.1 m (3 ft) • WEIGHT 2–4 kg (5–10 lb) •
FOOD Meat • YOUNG Eggs • LIVED Late Jurassic 150–146 million years ago

Theropods

Compsognathus is one of the smallest dinosaurs found in Jurassic rocks. It was very lightly built, with a small, pointed head and many small teeth. Its head was less than 10 cm (4 in) long. The tail accounted for more than half the total length of the animal. *Compsognathus* walked and ran on its hind legs and used its hands to hold food.

Some people think *Compsognathus* had two fingers, like *Tyrannosaurus*

(see page 64); others believe that it had three and was not that closely related to the 'Tyrant Lizard'.

Compsognathus lived at the same time and in the same place as *Archaeopteryx* (see page 115), the first bird. Beautifully preserved fossils have been uncovered from the lithographic limestone quarries of southwest Germany and sometimes it is difficult to tell which bones belong to *Compsognathus* and which

to *Archaeopteryx*. 'Pretty Jaw' has what look like some primitive feathers but most palaeontologists believe that *Compsognathus* was not the true ancestor of the first birds.

One fossil *Compsognathus* has been found with the bones of a small lizard inside it. The lizard seems to have been the little dinosaur's last meal.

Ornitholestes or-ni-tho-less-tees

Bird Robber

59

Saurischia • Theropoda • Tetanurae • Coelurosauria • Family: ?Ornitholestidae

FIRST DISCOVERED **1900** • FOUND **North America: USA** • LENGTH **c.2 m (6½ ft)** • WEIGHT **12 kg (26.5 lb)**
• FOOD **Meat** • YOUNG **Eggs** • LIVED **Late Jurassic 155–147 million years ago**

Although *Ornitholestes* has been known since 1900, it is uncertain which other dinosaurs were its nearest relatives. In many ways, it is similar to *Coelophysis* (see page 39) and *Compsognathus* (see page 58),
but there are important differences in its skull, its arms and its hands. *Ornitholestes*'s skull is more robust than that of the other two and it has more and bigger teeth. It also seems to have had a more powerful bite so that it could hold on to quite large prey. Its arms were big in relation to its body and its hands had three fingers, the first being shorter than the other two. The longer arm and
slender fingers of *Ornitholestes* are just what we would expect from an egg stealer or from a hunter that snatched at lizards, small dinosaurs or birds.

Currently, most scientists think that *Ornitholestes* is likely to be a member of the manuraptor group of dinosaurs, which may include birds!

Theropods

Caudipteryx caw-dip-ter-rix
Tail Feathers

Saurischia • Theropoda • Tetanurae • Manuraptora • Family: Caudipteridae
FIRST DISCOVERED 1998 • FOUND **Asia: China** • LENGTH *c*.1 m (3 ft) • WEIGHT **3–5 kg (6½–11 lb)**
• FOOD **Meat** • YOUNG **Eggs** • LIVED **Early Cretaceous 145–140 million years ago**

The mysteries surrounding the close links between birds and dinosaurs were unravelled during the last quarter of the 20th century. The similarities and differences between *Compsognathus* (see page 58) and *Archaeopteryx* (see page 115) were studied, and a dinosaur family tree for today's birds was created with confidence. Whether or not *Archaeopteryx* actually flew was debated furiously for several years. Surely the ancestors of the birds would be scaly, whereas only true birds would have feathers? Not so! In 1998 fossils of the first feathered, bird-like dinosaurs began to turn up in China.

Caudipteryx belongs to a branch of the theropod family tree that did not evolve into birds. But the discovery of this small, delicately built theropod with its modified, wing-like arm strengthened our belief in the idea that birds had evolved from theropods. *Caudipteryx* also had a well-developed wishbone, essential for the attachment of flight muscles in birds. Some reconstructions of *Caudipteryx* are quite bizarre, showing colourful wing and tail feathers spread out rather like those of a displaying cock pheasant.

Troödon troo-uh-don

Tooth That Wounds

Saurischia • Theropoda • Tetanurae • Manuraptora • Family: Troödontidae

FIRST DESCRIBED 1856 • FOUND **North America: Canada, USA** • LENGTH **c.3 m (10 ft)**
• WEIGHT **50 kg (110 lb)** • FOOD **Meat** • YOUNG **Eggs** • LIVED **Late Cretaceous 80–72 million years ago**

Troödon was a relatively small thero-pod that evolved very late in the history of the dinosaurs. Its fossils have been found in the north-western part of North America, in the Judith River Formation of Alberta and in rocks of the same age in Montana, Wyoming and perhaps Alaska.

Troödon had large eyes and one of the largest brains of all dinosaurs. Its senses may have been quite out-standing and it was probably a night hunter. It is difficult to measure intelligence when all you have to go on is an empty braincase but, as dinosaurs go, *Troödon* would probably have been quite clever!

Only fragments of the skull have been found but, uniquely, the lower jaw was armed with more than 30 saw-edged teeth on each side. Overall, the body was moderately well built, with a medium-length neck and long tail. The arms were short, each bearing a three-fingered hand. Nests of eggs thought to have belonged to *Troödon* are quite com-mon in the Egg Mountain area of Montana. One nest has been found to contain the remains of part of an adult and an egg with an embryo.

Theropods

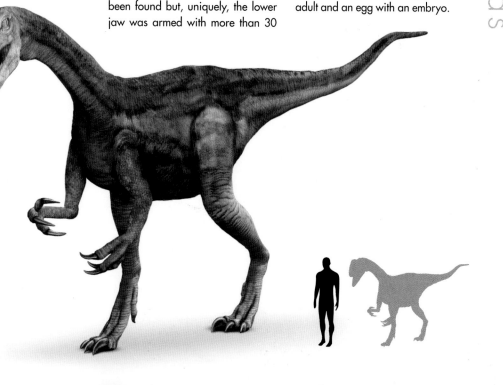

Alioramus al-ee-oh-ray-mus
Different Branch

Saurischia • Theropoda • Tetanurae • Manuraptoriformes • Family: Tyrannosauridae

First Described 1976 • Found Asia: Mongolia • Length c.6 m (20 ft) • Weight 1–1.5 t • Food Meat
• Young Eggs • Lived Late Cretaceous 73–68 million years ago

Alioramus is known from a single, incomplete skull and a few bones from the feet. It was discovered in the Ingenii Höövör valley of the Bayankhongor area of Mongolia. Because this is a faraway land for many, it was named *Alioramus remotus*.

The closest relatives of this medium-sized theropod are the tyrannosaurids, including the *Tarbosaurus* (see page 63) and *Tyrannosaurus rex* (see page 64). In contrast to these Late Cretaceous monsters, *Alioramus* had a rather flatter skull and a row of six bony knobs along the snout. The skull was only 70 cm (28 in) long. *Alioramus* had many more teeth in its jaws than those of its larger cousins and it seems to represent a separate branch on the tyrannosaurid family tree.

Some people say that the remains from Mongolia are from a young animal (juvenile). They also say that the braincase of *Alioramus* is more like *Tarbosaurus*'s than that of *T. rex*. This would seem to be logical because *Tarbosaurus* is also found in Cretaceous rocks of Mongolia.

Tarbosaurus tar-boh-saw-rus

Alarming Lizard

Saurischia • Theropoda • Tetanurae • Manuraptoriformes • Family: Tyrannosauridae

FIRST DISCOVERED **1955** • FOUND **Asia: Mongolia** • LENGTH **c.13 m (43 ft)** • WEIGHT **5–7 t** • FOOD **Meat**
• YOUNG **Eggs** • LIVED **Late Cretaceous 73–68 million years ago**

At first, scientists identified two species of this giant theropod from Mongolia. One of these is still called *Tarbosaurus efremov* but the other has had its name changed twice – first to *Tarbosaurus battar* and then to *Jenghizkhan battar*. Genghis (or Jenghiz) Khan (1162–1227) was the Mongol conqueror of most of Asia and Eastern Europe and his name conjures up terror in the minds of many people. It is a good name for a massive theropod that would have caused panic as it tracked a herd of sauropods across the open landscape of Mongolia around 70 million years ago.

Tarbosaurus was the Asian equivalent of *Tyrannosaurus rex*. It had a great head, huge, saw-edged teeth, a short neck, a very strong back and a long tail. The hind legs and hips were strongly built, and the front of the animal was balanced perfectly by the length and weight of the tail. As with *Tyrannosaurus* (see page 64), the arms of *Tarbosaurus* were ridiculously short and each had two quite long fingers and the trace of a third on the inside of the hand.

Theropods

Tyrannosaurus *tie-ran-oh-saw-rus*

Tyrant Lizard

Saurischia • Theropoda • Tetanurae • Family: Tyrannosauridae

FIRST DISCOVERED **1902** • FOUND **North America: USA** • LENGTH *c.*12 m (40 ft) • WEIGHT **4–7 t** • FOOD **Meat**
• YOUNG **Eggs** • LIVED **Late Cretaceous 70–66 million years ago**

Until fairly recently *Tyrannosaurus rex* was thought to be the largest meat-eating hunter ever to have stalked the Earth. The discovery of *Carcharodontosaurus* (see page 56), *Giganotosaurus* (see page 57), and *Jenghizkhan* (see page 63) have challenged its status as 'king of the tyrant lizards'. Strangely, though, *Tyrannosaurus* is still the dinosaur we think of when asked to name a gigantic meat eater. Typically, it had a very large head with powerful jaws and huge saw-edged teeth capable of crunching through bones. The head was 1.5 m (5 ft) long and the biggest teeth are 30 cm (1 ft) from the point to the base of the root. *T. rex* has been described, accurately, as the most efficient killer to have appeared in the fossil record.

There are beautiful exhibits at the Natural History Museum in New York and the Field Museum in Chicago. In the Field Museum, 'Sue', the most expensive dinosaur ever, is on display. In 1997, she was bought for $8.4 million at Sotheby's in New York. The exhibits in New York and Chicago show how well balanced *Tyrannosaurus* was and how threatening it would have been to even the largest, best-armoured dinosaurs. Massive scars on *Tyrannosaurus*

bones were probably the result of tyrannosaurids fighting among themselves. Even the dung of *T. rex* was on a giant scale: a fossil dropping 43 cm (17 in) long was discovered in Saskatchewan, Canada, in 1998!

Gallimimus gal-ee-mime-us

Chicken Mimic

Saurischia • Theropoda • Tetanurae • Ornithomimosauria • Family: Ornithomimidae

FIRST DESCRIBED 1972 • FOUND **Asia: Mongolia** • LENGTH **c.4 m (13 ft)** • WEIGHT **400 kg (880 lb)**
• FOOD **Plants, insects, meat, eggs** • YOUNG **Eggs** • LIVED **Late Cretaceous 80–68 million years ago**

Gallimimus was the largest of the 'chicken-mimic' dinosaurs. It had a small, toothless head, a very long neck, long arms and very long fingers. Overall, it looked like an ostrich without feathers. *Gallimimus* was a very fast runner – some scientists have suggested that it could reach speeds of up to 60 mph (almost 100 kph). Others think that 40 mph (nearly 65 kph) was much more likely. *Gallimimus* probably ate anything it could catch, in other words it was an omnivore. Small mammals, reptiles, insects and even plants may have been included in its diet. It could also pick up eggs from a nest or dig out tiny creatures from their burrows. It may even have had a filter system in its mouth to sieve insects from mouthfuls of muddy water.

Gallimimus probably lived in fairly large groups and is known to have coexisted with duck-billed dinosaurs and the dreaded tyrannosaurids. It was first discovered by a Polish-Mongolian Expedition in the Bayshin Tsav region of south-eastern Mongolia. There are two known species, *Gallimimus bullatus* and *Gallimimus mongoliensis*.

Theropods

Struthiomimus stroo-thee-oh-mime-us

Ostrich Mimic

Saurischia • Theropoda • Tetanurae • Ornithomimosauria • Family: Ornithomimidae

FIRST DISCOVERED 1902 • FOUND **North America: Canada** • LENGTH **c.4 m (13 ft)** • WEIGHT **350 kg (770 lb)** • FOOD **Meat, plants** • YOUNG **Eggs** • LIVED **Late Cretaceous 80–72 million years ago**

Theropods

Struthiomimus was a smaller version of *Gallimimus* (see page 65) and, again, resembles a featherless ostrich. It had a small head with a toothless beak. The neck and tail were very long. The skull was lightly built, with huge openings for the eyes. *Struthiomimus* had very good eyesight and was in all likelihood quite intelligent. It fed on insects, small reptiles and probably plants. *Struthiomimus*'s large eyes may have given it stereoscopic vision, so that it had a three-dimensional view of the world. This would have allowed the 'Ostrich Mimic' to judge distances accurately and to hunt at dusk or even during the night.

Like many other dinosaurs, *Struthiomimus* had small stones in its gizzard (the part of a bird's stomach which grinds food – in this case, tough plant material). It is known from Alberta in western Canada and, along with 30 or so other dinosaurs, is part of one of the world's best exhibitions at the Tyrrell Museum in Drumheller.

Falcarius fal-car-ee-us
Sickle Maker

Saurischia • Theropoda • Tetanurae • Oviraptorosauria • Therizinosauroidea
• Family: Therizinosauridae

FIRST DISCOVERED 1999 • FOUND North America: United States • LENGTH c.4 m (13 ft) • WEIGHT 800 kg
(1,760 lb) • FOOD ?Meat, plants • YOUNG Eggs • LIVED Early Cretaceous 125–120 million years ago

In an age when rare fossils are sold for huge sums of money, the story of *Falcarius* is truly amazing. It reads like a detective story. The original discovery was made in a protected area in 1999. The fossil hunter, who did not have permission to be there, intended to sell his find to the highest bidder. Rumours about the new discovery gradually leaked out and James Kirkland of the Utah Geological Survey led a search for the site.

Stealing fossils from a protected site is a serious offence in the USA and, fearing a long jail sentence, the man who found the site decided to help Kirkland in his search. His sentence was reduced but he still went to jail! The story is one of intrigue and determination, but the result was well worth the effort. Kirkland literally uncovered a graveyard of these new dinosaurs. Over 1,700 bones were collected, the vast majority of which were from the skeletons of *Falcarius*. It is likely that poisoning at a gas-rich waterhole killed the animals.

Falcarius is now known to be a very primitive member of a family halfway between meat eaters – such as *Velociraptor* (see page 77) – and *Beipiaosaurus*, a plant eater. It had leaf-shaped teeth typical of a plant eater, a long neck, strong, flexible arms and strong, quite short legs. It was broad at the hips and could have had a larger than normal gut, typical of other plant eaters.

Theropods

Alxasaurus alks-ah-saw-rus

Alxa Desert Lizard

Saurischia • Theropoda • Tetanurae • Therizinosauroidea • Family: Alxasauridae

FIRST DISCOVERED 1994 • FOUND **Asia: Mongolia** • LENGTH **c.4 m (13 ft)** • WEIGHT **400 kg (880 lb)** • FOOD **Meat, ?pla**
• YOUNG **Eggs** • LIVED **Early Cretaceous 112–105 million years ago**

Alxasaurus is often described as the most complete theropod so far found in Asia. It is a rather strange-looking creature which, in some ways, resembles an early prosauropod. It is not a sauropod, though. Most of its characteristics suggest that it was a very primitive therizinosaur. The therizinosaurs were a group of medium to large theropod dinosaurs that had small heads, relatively long arms and thin, moderately curved claws on each hand. In primitive forms the claws were about 15 cm (6 in) long but later therizinosaurs had flattened claws almost 1 m (3 ft) in length.

Alxasaurus had a relatively short tail and a long neck, and was very robustly built at the shoulders. It had more than 40 teeth in the lower jaw. While feeding, the animal may have leaned backwards on its hind legs and tail, reaching upwards to grasp leaves. When down on all four limbs, it may have dug into the ground in search of insects or succulent roots.

Therizinosaurus ther-ih-zin-oh-saw-rus

Scythe Lizard

Saurischia • Theropoda • Tetanurae • Therizinosauroidea • Family: Therizinosauridae

FIRST DISCOVERED **1948** • FOUND **Asia: Mongolia** • LENGTH **c.8 m (26 ft)** • WEIGHT **2–4 t**
• FOOD **?Insects, plants** • YOUNG **Eggs** • LIVED **Late Cretaceous 80–70 million years ago**

Not much is known about *Therizinosaurus*. Only some claws, a tooth and a few pieces of limb bone have been retrieved from the wastes of the southern Gobi Desert of Mongolia. The claws, however, are simply enormous and reconstructions of this animal are sometimes quite bizarre! Imagine a huge feathered dinosaur with 1-m (3-ft) claws on its hands, and you can picture one of the strangest animals ever to have walked on Earth.

At first, it was thought that *Therizinosaurus* was a turtle, because the flattened, curved claws looked like the ribs of a giant sea-going leathery turtle. During the 1960s and 1980s, however, some new finds from Asia showed that the claws belonged to a group of dinosaurs with long to very long arms which may have been covered in primitive feather-like structures.

How did this giant live and what were the claws for?

Some scientists suggest that the animal used its great claws for cutting and slashing at the soft underbelly of large prey. Others believe that they were perfect tools for digging into termite mounds. Or perhaps they were used like scissors to cut shrubs and bushes. Meat eater or vegetarian? The mystery of *Therizinosaurus* remains unsolved.

Theropods

Incisivosaurus in-siz-iv-oh-saw-rus

Incisor Lizard

Saurischia • Theropoda • Tetanurae • Oviraptorosauria • Family: Oviraptoridae

FIRST DESCRIBED 2002 • FOUND Asia: China • LENGTH c.90 cm (3 ft) • WEIGHT 4 kg (8½ lb) • FOOD Plants
• YOUNG Eggs • LIVED Early Cretaceous 120–115 million years ago

Theropods

Incisivosaurus has often been called the 'buck-toothed' dinosaur. It is only known from a single skull and one neck bone, but still the 'Incisor Lizard' fascinates us. From the few fossils we have, we can see that the skull is long but, unlike other beaked, oviraptorid dinosaurs, such as *Oviraptor* (the 'Egg Stealer', see page 72), the front of mouth contains many sharp teeth. These are similar to the teeth found in modern rodents (rats and mice, for instance). They are clearly not suitable for gripping eggs, and most scientists think that *Incisivosaurus* gnawed on pinecones and other tough plant material. There were more teeth at the sides of the jaws which the little dinosaur could have used to grind and crush the food.

When *Incisivosaurus* is illustrated, it is often shown with a coat of primitive feathers, but we cannot be sure that this was there. It seems likely that *Incisivosaurus* is a specialized, maybe primitive, form of the small egg-stealing dinosaurs that evolved during the Late Cretaceous.

Ingenia in-gen-ee-ah

Able or Talented

Saurischia • Theropoda • Tetanurae • Oviraptorosauria • Family ?Igenidae

FIRST DESCRIBED 1981 • FOUND Asia: Mongolia • LENGTH c.1.6 m (5 ft 3 in) • WEIGHT 30 kg (66 lb)
• FOOD Meat, Plants • YOUNG Eggs • LIVED Late Cretaceous 82–75 million years ago

Many dinosaurs are known only from a few fossil fragments, but six skeletons of *Ingenia* have been unearthed in the Gobi Desert of Mongolia. Several are complete. They are more robustly built than the skeletons of other similar dinosaurs and there is no trace of a head crest. The skull was quite deep with a big beak. It was about 11 cm (4½ in) long. A horny shield probably covered the upper and lower jaws and there were no teeth whatsoever. As it is in turtles and birds, the horny beak would have been ideal for snipping or cutting all sorts of potential food.

Ingenia has a well-developed wishbone rather like *Archaeopteryx* (see page 115). The neck and tail are quite long and the arms are approximately half the length of the legs. In contrast to its cousin, *Oviraptor* (see page 72), *Ingenia* had hands where all three fingers were rather short and stubby. This suggests that *Ingenia* was adapted to a different way of life.

Theropods

Oviraptor ove-ee-rap-tor

Egg Stealer

Saurischia • Theropoda • Tetanurae • Oviraptorosauria • Family: Oviraptoridae

FIRST DESCRIBED **1924** FOUND **Asia: Mongolia** • LENGTH **c.2 m (6½ ft)** WEIGHT **30 kg (66 lb)**
• FOOD **Meat, eggs** • YOUNG **Eggs** LIVED **Late Cretaceous 82–70 million years ago**

There are two known species of *Oviraptor*: *O. philoceratops* and *O. mongoliensis*. Both were quite small, two-legged creatures and both have head crests. The crest of *O. philoceratops* had a rather square profile whereas that of *O. mongoliensis* was rounder, with a mass of bone above the beak. The crests look like the comb on a cockerel's head. Some reconstructions show a small horn and no crest.

Oviraptor and its close relatives were common animals in Asia and North America during the Late Cretaceous. They were specialized nest raiders that stole eggs and young from the nests of the small horned dinosaur, *Protoceratops* (see page 86). *Oviraptor* also laid eggs and there is evidence to show that these dinosaurs were protective parents. An *Oviraptor* has been found sitting on a nest with its eggs carefully nestled in its arms. It died during a sandstorm.

The 'Egg Stealer' was lightly built with long legs and long-clawed toes. It probably had a stiffened tail, perhaps with feathers. Agility and speed were essential if *Oviraptor* was to avoid direct confrontation with an enraged parent.

Deinonychus die-noh-nye-kus

Terrible Claw

Saurischia • Theropoda • Tetanurae • Eumanuraptora • Deinonychosauria
• Family: Dromaeosauridae

FIRST DISCOVERED **1964** • FOUND **North America: USA** • LENGTH **c.3 m (10 ft)** • WEIGHT **50 kg (110 lb)**
• FOOD **Meat** • YOUNG **Eggs** • LIVED **Early Cretaceous 124–110 million years ago**

Fossils of 'Terrrible Claw' have been found in the western states of the United States. The remains of nine skeletons have been unearthed from the Morrison Formation of Montana, Oklahoma and Utah. There is doubt about finds from Maryland, and one from Korea is now thought more likely to be a *Velociraptor* (see page 77). *Deinonychus* and *Velociraptor* are very closely related and seem to be found in what were the same sorts of environments in North America and Asia. In the United States, *Deinonychus* has been found with freshwater turtles, crocodiles and plant-eating sauropods. Forest glades bordered small lakes, and the herds of sauropods provided many opportunities as food for this near perfect predator.

Deinonychus was fairly small, with a large head, short neck and stiffened tail. The arms were strong, with three long-clawed fingers for slashing and tearing at its prey. The hind limbs were also potential weapons of destruction with a huge 13-cm (5-in) movable claw on the second toe of each. While this fearsome dinosaur was running, the claw was held off the ground, but in attack it would be rotated downwards and viciously driven home as the predator lunged or jumped at the terrified victim.

Theropods

Microraptor my-crow-rap-tor
Little Thief

Saurischia • Theropoda • Tetanurae • Manuraptora • Deinonychosauria • Family: Dromaeosauridae

FIRST DESCRIBED **2000** • FOUND **Asia: China** • LENGTH *c*.**50 cm (1¾ ft)** • WEIGHT **2–3 kg (5–7 lb)** • FOOD **Meat, insects** • YOUNG **Eggs** • LIVED **Early Cretaceous 128–126 million years ago**

As its name suggests, *Microraptor* was a very small dinosaur. In fact, it is the smallest adult theropod dinosaur ever found. It is also one of the strangest, as several aspects of it are typical of a *Troödon* (see page 61) while others are more like those of birds or bird-like dinosaurs. The teeth are particularly interesting:

from the front of the mouth to the back, they vary in shape, size and the amount of curve; some are saw-edged and others are not. The teeth at the front more closely resemble those of a bird-like dinosaur.

Microraptor had a very short body and the tail was stiffened by rod-shaped tendons. The limbs were delicately built, with three long and one much shorter claw on each foot.

Some scientists argue that the feet of *Microraptor* were adapted to climbing trees. The original, beautifully preserved fossil was discovered when a slab of rock was split open. When the two sides of the original slab were examined carefully, it became clear that *Microraptor* had a partial covering of feathers.

Utahraptor yoo-tar-rap-tor

Utah Raider

Saurischia • Theropoda • Tetanurae • Manuraptora • Deinonychosauria
• Family: Dromaeosauridae

FIRST DESCRIBED **1991** • FOUND **North America: USA, ?South America** • LENGTH **c.6.5 m (21 ft)**
• WEIGHT **1 t** • FOOD **Meat** • YOUNG **Eggs** • LIVED **Early Cretaceous 130–125 million years ago**

Like *Deinonychus* (see page 73) and *Microraptor* (see page 74), *Utahraptor* is a member of the dromaeosaurid family of theropod dinosaurs. Dromaeosaurs are the 'swift lizards', small to medium-sized hunters with excellent eyesight, relatively high intelligence and great agility. It is likely that they hunted in 'packs'. When the famous sickle-like claw was shown being unearthed in the film *Jurassic Park*, this was actually based on the discovery of *Utahraptor*.

Utahraptor is one of the largest dinosaurs of the dromaeosaurid family. It has a large head, narrow snout and straight lower jaw. The arms were robust with three long, clawed fingers on the hands. Interestingly, the hands could be rotated slightly at the wrist. The legs were very powerful and the second toe had developed into a huge sickle-shaped claw. A stiffened tail would have helped the animal keeps its balance. *Utahraptor* probably tracked and killed animals much larger than itself. An aged or wounded sauropod would have stood little chance against a pack of persistent predators attacking from all angles.

Dromaeosaurus dro-may-oh-saw-rus
Swift-running Lizard

Saurischia •Theropoda • Tetanurae • Manuraptora • Deinonychosauria
• Family: Dromaeosauridae

FIRST DESCRIBED 1922 • FOUND **North America: Canada: USA** • LENGTH **c.1.5 m (6½ ft)**
• WEIGHT **33 kg (66 lb)** • FOOD **Meat** • YOUNG **Eggs** • LIVED **Late Cretaceous 80–71 million years ago**

Theropods

Dromaeosaurus has been described as 'the original raptor'. It was first discovered in the dinosaur-rich Judith River deposits of Alberta in Canada, but further material has since been unearthed in Montana in the USA. *Dromaeosaurus* was a small, very agile meat eater. However, it had quite a large brain-case and big eyes. The mouth was armed with numerous razor-sharp teeth that were serrated along the edges.

Although a lightweight, *Dromaeosaurus* was quite well built, with long arms and fingers that ended in vicious, curved claws. The hind limbs were also quite long, with a well-developed, dagger-like claw on the second toe of each foot. It is unlikely that this little dinosaur would attack animals much larger than itself, but

if it hunted in packs then the results would be quite devastating. The dromaeosaurs were noted for their long, stiff tails. Together with good sight and a relatively high intelligence, they were effectively the wild dogs or wolves of the Age of Dinosaurs.

Velociraptor vel-oss-ee-rap-tor

Fast Robber

Saurischia • Theropoda • Tetanurae • Manuraptora • Deinonychosauria
• Family Dromaeosauridae

FIRST DESCRIBED 1924 • FOUND Asia: Russia, Mongolia, China • LENGTH c.2 m (6½ ft) • WEIGHT 15 kg (33 lb)
• FOOD Meat • YOUNG Eggs • LIVED Late Cretaceous 70–65 million years ago

Several skeletons of this small aggressive theropod have been found across Asia. They include adults and young. *Velociraptor* was brought to life in the film *Jurassic Park* when it pitted its wits against a host of terrified humans. Typically, *Velociraptor* was an agile, fast-running hunter. It had quite a long, narrow head with very sharp, backward-curving teeth. In modern animals, such as poisonous snakes, teeth like these enable the predator to hold on tightly to a struggling victim.

Actual *Velociraptors* are much smaller than the ones that starred in the film, and their tails were rigid rather than whip-like. One of the specimens found in Mongolia seems to have died during a raid on the nest of the small-horned *Protoceratops* (see page 86). The two animals are locked in an embrace of death and the protective mother probably surprised the cunning raider as it attempted to steal her eggs or hatchlings. Strangely, both were entombed forever by a desert sand-storm, the dagger-like claws of *Velociraptor* still deeply buried in the remains of *Protoceratops*.

Theropods

Heterodontosaurus het-ur-oh-dont-oh-saw-rus
Different-toothed Lizard

Ornithischia • Genaria • Cerapoda • Family: Heterodontosauridae

FIRST DESCRIBED **1962** • FOUND **Africa: South Africa** • LENGTH **c.1.2 m (4 ft)** • WEIGHT **9 kg (20 lb)**
• FOOD **Plants** • YOUNG **Eggs** • LIVED **Early Jurassic 150–146 million years ago**

Ornithischians

Heterodontosaurus is one of the earliest ornithischian, or bird-hipped, dinosaurs. It is known from a complete skeleton and parts of a jaw. The skull is unique and has three types of teeth. The front teeth were sharp and used for cutting and snipping, whereas those at the back were broader and flatter and were used to grind tough vegetation before it was swallowed. These back teeth had a thick coat of enamel which would have prevented them from wearing out quickly. The third kind of teeth were tusk-like, resembling the canines of a dog.

Scientists think that *Heterodontosaurus* probably had fleshy cheeks or 'pouches', which were used to hold extra food. As the animal ground up some food with its teeth, the muscular cheeks would help by pushing the food from side to side to produce a chewing action. We are not sure what the canine teeth were used for but they may have allowed *Heterodontosaurus* to dig up roots. It ran on its two strong back legs and had well-developed arms.

Stegoceras steg-o-ser-as

Roof Horn

Ornithischia • Genaria • Cerapoda • Marginocephalia • Pachycephalosauria • Family: Pachycephalosauridae

FIRST DESCRIBED **1902** • FOUND **North America: Canada** • LENGTH *c.*2.5 m (8¼ ft) • WEIGHT **70 kg (154 lb)** • FOOD **Plants** • YOUNG **Eggs** • LIVED **Late Cretaceous 76–68 million years ago**

Stegoceras is a member of the same family as *Pachycephalosaurus* (see page 81), the 'Thick-headed Lizard', but it was only one-third the size of its giant cousin. One of the main family characteristics was the greatly thickened roof of the skull. Scientists have debated why the skull was thickened, and most think that males fought one another over territory. The larger the male and the thicker his skull, the stronger and more mature he was. Numerous skulls of *Stegoceras* have been discovered and they show a range of ages, the older animals having the thickest skull roofs. Modern-day mountain sheep and goats have a similar skull thickening. It is likely that *Stegoceras* lived in upland areas.

Only one poorly preserved skeleton has been discovered, and the evidence suggests that *Stegoceras* was quite lightly built, with short arms and strong legs. Compared to some theropods, the hands and feet of *Stegoceras* were quite primitive. The hands have five fingers, whereas the feet have three moderately long toes and an inner toe that is reduced to just a spur.

Cerapods

Homalocephale ho-mal-oh-seph-ah-le

Even Head

Ornithischia •Genaria • Cerapoda • Marginocephalia • Pachycephalosauria
• Family: Homalocephalidae

First Described **1974** • Found **Asia: Mongolia** • Length **c.3 m (9¾ ft)** • Weight **225 kg (496 lb)**
• Food **Plants** • Young **Eggs** • Lived **Late Cretaceous 76–68 million years ago**

This odd, rather small dinosaur was found in Mongolia in 1969. It was the first bone-headed dinosaur to be discovered with its skull. Until it was found, the bone-headed dinosaurs were known only through parts of skulls. This was probably because they are likely to have lived in dry, upland areas where the more delicate bones of the skeletons were destroyed before they could be buried and preserved.

The skull of *Homalocephale* was 15 cm (6 in) thick, but unlike that of *Pachycephalosaurus* (see page 81) the skull roof was flat. Most scientists attribute this feature to a herding way of life with the large males using their heads as battering rams during battles over territory or females.

The spine of *Homalocephale* was quite rigid and the hips broadly spaced. These features, together with widely spaced back legs and a rigid tail, helped *Homalocephale* withstand the enormous shockwaves generated in battle. It has also been suggested that some of these features were associated with the birth of live young.

Pachycephalosaurus pack-ee-seph-ah-loh-saw-rus
Thick-headed Lizard

Ornithischia • Genaria • Cerapoda • Marginocephalia • Pachycephalosauria
• Family: Pachycephalosauridae

First Described **1943** • Found **North America: USA** • Length **c.8 m (26 ft)** • Weight **1 t**
• Food **Plants** • Young **Eggs** • Lived **Late Cretaceous 76–68 million years ago**

Pachycephalosaurus is known, only poorly, from Wyoming, South Dakota and Montana in the western United States. It was one of the largest of the dome- or flat-headed dinosaurs, with the thick, bony mass at the top of its head up to 20 cm (8 in) thick. As with other pachycephalosaurs, this strengthening and thickening of the skull protected it during fights for territory, dominance of the herd or mating partners. The bigger the male, the bigger the domed skull and the more likely that he would be the victor in battle.

Only one good fossil *Pachycephalosaurus* skull has been found, as well as several skull roofs. The reconstruction of the rest of the animal is based on comparing it with related dinosaurs and on informed guesswork. A detailed comparison is now possible because a reasonably complete skeleton of the closely related *Stygimoloch* was found in 1995. Each animal had a bony ornament over the snout and rear of the head, but in *Stygimoloch* the rear bony swellings had developed into long horns. Both animals ran on two legs. They probably had relatively short arms and a long, stiffened tail.

Cerapods

Psittacosaurus sit-tak-oh- saw-rus

Parrot Lizard

Ornithischia • Genaria • Cerapoda • Marginocephalia • Ceratopsia • Family: Psittacosauridae

FIRST DESCRIBED 1923 • FOUND Asia: China, Mongolia, Thailand • LENGTH *c.*2 m (6½ ft) • WEIGHT 70 kg (154 lb) • FOOD Plants • YOUNG Eggs • LIVED Early Cretaceous 125–100 million years ago

Psittacosaurus is a small, primitive, horned-faced dinosaur. It is thought to be have been related to the small ornithopod *Hypsilophodon* (see page 103). The horned-faced dinosaurs probably evolved from an ornithopod ancestor similar to a hypsilophodontid. The tell-tale presence of a small beak-like bone at the front of the skull of *Psittacosaurus* makes it one the earliest relatives of giants such as *Styracosaurus* (see page 87) and *Triceratops* (see page 89).

Nine species of *Psittacosaurus* have been found in the Early Cretaceous rocks of Asia, and the remains of over a hundred individuals have been collected so far. This is an enormous number and shows how well this small dinosaur was adapted to its surroundings. Its robust parrot-like beak suggests that it fed on tough plant material, which

it gathered while standing on its hind limbs. *Psittacosaurus* had fairly long arms, with four fingers on each hand. The hind limbs were longer and more robust, with three toes and an inner spur on the feet.

Leptoceratops lep-toe-ser-ah-tops

Slender Horned Face

Ornithischia • Genaria • Cerapoda • Marginocephalia • Ceratopsoidea
• Family: uncertain

FIRST DESCRIBED **1914** • FOUND **North America: USA, Canada** • LENGTH **c.2–3 m (6½–10 ft)**
• WEIGHT **180 kg (400 lb)** • FOOD **Plants** • YOUNG **Eggs** • LIVED **Late Cretaceous 82–80 million years ago**

Leptoceratops is one of those strange creatures that are difficult to place accurately within a given family. It has similarities to *Psittacosaurus* (see page 82) and to *Protoceratops* (see page 86), and it may be descended from the first and the ancestor of the second. Like *Psittacosaurus*, the head had no horns, but it did have traces of a bony frill. The frill lacked the openings found in *Protoceratops* and the larger *Triceratops* (see page 89), however. The creature could move on two or on four legs depending on whether it was running or simply feeding. All the bigger, frilled ceratopsians walked on all fours.

Apart from a horn-covered beak at the front of the mouth, *Leptoceratops* had some comparatively small cheek teeth. It probably spent quite lot of time clipping at soft plant material, which was then ground up towards the back of the mouth. Interestingly, the roots of the jaw teeth of *Leptoceratops* had only a single root, whereas those of *Triceratops* had two.

Cerapods

Pachyrhinosaurus pak-ee-rhino-saw-rus

Thick-nosed Lizard

Ornithischia • Genaria • Cerapoda • Marginocephalia • Ceratopsoidea • Family: ?Ceratopsidae

FIRST DESCRIBED 1950 • FOUND North America: Canada • LENGTH c.6 m (20 ft) • WEIGHT 2 t • FOOD Plants • YOUNG Eggs • LIVED Late Cretaceous 70–66 million years ago

Cerapods

Twelve or more skulls and some disconnected bones have been found in the western states of Canada. The form of the body, therefore, has been built up by comparing the known remains with those of other horned and frilled dinosaurs. Instead of a nose horn, *Pachyrhinosaurus* had a large, bony bump on its nose. It was probably used for defence and during the fierce battles among the dominant males fighting to protect their territory and breeding partners. Head-butting and pushing would have been the chosen battlefield strategy.

Pachyrhinosaurus had a short frill at the back of its head similar to that of *Triceratops* (see page 89). During Late Cretaceous times, large herds of horned dinosaurs roamed the open lands of the western area of the North American continent. They were constantly on the lookout for *Tyrannosaurus rex* (see page 64) and, when spooked, were capable of running at speeds of more than 12 mph (20 kph). Even the 'Tyrant Lizard' would get out of the way of a stampede of these formidable creatures.

Pentaceratops pent-ah-ser-ah-tops

Five-horned Face

Ornithischia • Genaria • Cerapoda • Marginocephalia • Ceratopsoidea
• Family: ?Ceratopsidae

FIRST DESCRIBED **1923** • FOUND **North America** • LENGTH **c.8 m (26 ft)** • WEIGHT **2.5 t** • FOOD **Plants**
• YOUNG **Eggs** • LIVED **Late Cretaceous 72–68 million years ago**

The recent discovery of a skull about 3 m (10 ft) long, gives *Pentaceratops* the prize for having the biggest head of any dinosaur. Nine skulls and several complete skeletons reveal that this giant plant eater was 4 m (13 ft) tall. *Pentaceratops* had five horns, one on the nose, one above each eye and one on each cheek. The cheek horns were small and were really just thickened cheekbones – they lacked the horn core typical of the nose and brow horns. The horns were arranged to give the best possible protection against giant hunters.

They protected the eyes and the face, and the huge shield stopped predators from biting and cutting the all-important neck muscles.

It is likely that large herds of these horned dinosaurs roamed the Late Cretaceous plains of New Mexico and Colorado. They were grazers, and their lifestyle probably resembled the way of life of modern African rhinoceroses.

Cerapods

Protoceratops pro-toe-ser-ah-tops

First Horned Face

Ornithischia • Genaria • Cerapoda • Marginocephalia • Neoceratopsoidea • Family: Protoceratopsidae

FIRST DESCRIBED 1923 • FOUND Asia; North America: Canada • LENGTH c.3 m (10 ft) • WEIGHT 230 kg (507 lb)• FOOD Plants • YOUNG Eggs • LIVED Late Cretaceous 82–78 million years ago

Most dinosaurs are known from a few bones or perhaps one or two complete skeletons. Hundreds of skeletons of *Protoceratops* have been discovered in the Gobi Desert of Mongolia. Two sites are particularly interesting. The first is known as the Flaming Cliff, because of the vivid red colour of the rocks that entomb *Protoceratops* and other dinosaur remains. The other site is called Tugrigiin Shiree, and is where *Protoceratops* and *Velociraptor* (see page 77) were discovered in mortal combat.

Compared with monsters such as *Triceratops* (see page 89), *Protoceratops* was quite small and had no horn. It walked on all fours and its neck was protected from attack by a well-developed shield. The front limbs were shorter than the back legs. Because of the huge number of *Protoceratops* skeletons that have been found, scientists have been able to identify differences between males and females. Overall, the males were much more robust, with larger, higher shields and a sizeable bump over the snout. The females were lighter in weight and their skeletons were less heavily built. Another information bonus from the discovery of so many skeletons is the fact that *Protoceratops* was a social creature and a good parent.

Cerapods

Styracosaurus sty-rack-oh-saw-rus

Spiked Lizard

Ornithischia • Genaria • Cerapoda • Marginocephalia • Ceratopsoidea • Family: Ceratopsidae

FIRST DESCRIBED **1913** • FOUND **North America: Canada, USA** • LENGTH **c.5.5 m (18 ft)** • WEIGHT **3 t** • FOOD **Plants** • YOUNG **Eggs** • LIVED **Late Cretaceous 80–66 million years ago**

This spectacular horned dinosaur stood 2 m (6½ ft) tall. It was like a giant rhinoceros except that the bony frill at the back of the skull was adorned with six long spines. In addition it had a tall, straight nasal horn and two bony spikes just below and to the sides of the eyes. Together, these gave *Styracosaurus* a lot of protection from attack by a giant predator. The tallest spines grew on either side of a central dip in the frill and they would have made even giants the size of *Albertosaurus* or *T. rex* (see page 64) think twice about attacking them. *Styracosaurus* lived in the western area of North America, including Montana, and in Alberta, Canada.

From the various skeletons discovered in Alberta, scientists have suggested that the heads of juveniles were very similar to those of adults although the spines and horns got larger as they got older. It was the biggest males that had the most spectacular head shields.

Cerapods

Torosaurus tore-oh-saw-rus

Bull Lizard

Ornithischia • Genaria • Cerapoda • Marginocephalia • Ceratopsoidea
• Family: Ceratopsidae

FIRST DISCOVERED **1889** • FOUND **North America: USA, Canada** • LENGTH **c.8 m (26 ft)** • WEIGHT **6 t**
• FOOD **Plants** • YOUNG **Eggs** • LIVED **Late Cretaceous 70–66 million years ago**

Without doubt, *Torosaurus* is one of the largest horned dinosaurs ever found. It was almost 3 m (10 ft) tall and the head measured 3 m (10 ft) from the tip of the horned beak to the back edge of the long, broad frill. Unlike that of *Styracosaurus* (see page 87), the frill had no spines but there were two large, skin-covered openings that would have reduced its weight. *Torosaurus* was a close relative of *Triceratops* (see page 89). It had two very large, slightly curved brow horns over the eyes and a comparatively short horn over the snout. *Torosaurus*'s body was massive and its legs were very strongly built. Typically, its feet were broad and perhaps even padded. *Torosaurus*'s hips were strengthened by bony rods to withstand withering attacks from a giant meat eater.

This huge, horned dinosaur was to be found throughout the western states of America during the Late Cretaceous, and there have also been a few finds in Saskatchewan in Canada.

Cerapods

Triceratops try-ser-ah-tops

Three-horned Face

Ornithischia • Genaria • Cerapoda • Marginocephalia • Ceratopsoidea
• Family: Ceratopsidae

FIRST DISCOVERED **1889** • FOUND **North America: USA, Canada** • LENGTH **c.9 m (30 ft)** • WEIGHT **7 t**
• FOOD **Plants** • YOUNG **Eggs** • LIVED **Late Cretaceous 70–66 million years ago**

Triceratops rivals *Tyrannosaurus* (see page 64) and *Stegosaurus* (see page 101) for the title of best-known dinosaur. This gigantic horned beast was one the most prominent plant-eating dinosaurs of the Late Cretaceous period. It probably existed in large herds. Sixteen different kinds of *Triceratops* appeared over a period of three to four million years – in effect, a new species every 250,000 years.

The final form, *Triceratops horridus*, was the biggest and most advanced. It is possible that some of these different kinds are really just the males and females within a given group of animals. Typically, the nose horn of *T. horridus* was short but the brow horns were almost 1 m (3 ft)

high. It would have needed several predators to bring down a full-grown male, and there is little doubt that a lumbering charge from one or two of these normally gentle creatures would have seen off even the most determined predator.

Triceratops was one of the last dinosaurs to live on Earth.

Cerapods

Einiosaurus eye-nee-oh-saw-rus

Buffalo Lizard

Ornithischia • Genaria • Cerapoda • Marginocephalia • Ceratopsoidea • Family: Ceratopsidae

FIRST DESCRIBED **1995** • FOUND **North America: USA** • LENGTH *c.*6 m (20 ft) • WEIGHT **2.5 t** • FOOD **Plants** • YOUNG **Eggs** • LIVED **Late Cretaceous 84–71 million years ago**

Cerapods

Einiosaurus is a relatively new addition to the world of dinosaurs. It is known only from the state of Montana and, as its name suggests,

it was found in Native American Territory: the word *einio* is the Blackfoot people's word for 'buffalo'.

Einiosaurus was a large centrosaur type of horned dinosaur. The centrosaurs have a rather short face with a long horn over the nose area. If brow horns occur, they are short. In

Einiosaurus the long horn on the nose is flattened at the sides. Two large, curved spikes adorn the large frill of the 'Buffalo Lizard'; the total length of skull rarely exceeds 1.5 m (5 ft).

Only two or three good skulls of this herding animal have been found but hundreds of bones are known from the Dino Ridge Quarry in Glacier County, Montana. These fossils include bones of animals of different ages, although the skulls all belong to adults. It is likely that such a large accumulation of bones was the result of a catastrophic event, perhaps a mass drowning or a large-scale attack by predators.

Scelidosaurus ske-lid-oh-saw-rus

Limb Lizard

Ornithischia • Genasauria • Thyreophoroidea • Family: uncertain

FIRST DISCOVERED **1859** • FOUND **Europe: England; North America: USA** • LENGTH *c.* **4 m (13 ft)**
• WEIGHT **500 kg (1,100 lb)** • FOOD **Plants** • YOUNG **Eggs** • LIVED **Early Jurassic 196–183 million years ago**

Scelidosaurus is a problem! It was originally thought to be the first-known ornithischian (bird-hipped) dinosaur. In 1861, the famous English anatomist and palaeontologist Sir Richard Owen described skeletal remains discovered in Dorset, in the south west of England. Strangely, Owen made a big mistake – the material he described was a mixture of bones from a new dinosaur and from the giant meat eater *Megalosaurus* (see page 51).

Better material became available in 1893 and, in 1985, a new skeleton was discovered in Charmouth, also in Dorset. Together, these remains have provided scientists with sufficient evidence to show that *Scelidosaurus* was most probably a distant relative of the armoured dinosaurs or ankylosaurs. *Scelidosaurus* may also be related to the stegosaurs.

Recent reconstructions show that it had a small head and its mouth contained many small, leaf-shaped teeth. Its body was long and robust and the front legs were shorter than the back. *Scelidosaurus* had rather rounded feet with short toes. It was a plant eater. Remains of the animal have been found in rocks containing sea creatures. It is very unlikely that *Scelidosaurus* ever ventured too close to the sea; the best explanation is that it slipped into a fast-flowing river while feeding or during a violent storm.

Cerapods

Gargoyleosaurus gar-goil-oh-saw-rus
Gargoyle Lizard

Ornithischia • Genasauria • Thyreophoroidea • Eurypoda • Ankylosauria • Family: Ankylosauridae

FIRST DESCRIBED **1998** • FOUND **North America: USA** • LENGTH **c.3 m (10 ft)** • WEIGHT **1 t** • FOOD **Plants** • YOUNG **Eggs** • LIVED **Late Jurassic 154–146 million years ago**

Cerapods

Gargoyleosaurus reminded the people who discovered it of a gargoyle – one of those ugly carvings you sometimes see on cathedrals or churches. Actually, it looks much the same as many other armoured dinosaurs. *Gargoyleosaurus* is known from only one skull and an incomplete skeleton discovered in the dinosaur-rich Morrison Formation of Wyoming in the United States. The remains were found in Bone Cabin Quarry, near which is a small house built entirely of dinosaur bones.

Typical of its family, the ankylosaurs, *Gargoyleosaurus* had a beak-like snout, and the bones of the skull were fused together to withstand an attack. Its body armour was hollow, however. Unusually, too, it had teeth on the inside margins of both the upper and lower jaws. These are primitive features not seen in Cretaceous members of the ankylosaur family. The body armour was made up of many closely spaced, oval plates with prominent spines around the edge. Although it was a relatively small animal, *Gargoyleosaurus* had a strongly built, low-slung body which most meat eaters would have found difficult to turn over, to get at the soft underbelly.

Gastonia gas-tone-ee-ah

Named after Gaston

Ornithischia • Genasauria • Thyreophoroidea • Eurypoda • Ankylosauria
• Family: Ankylosauridae

FIRST DESCRIBED 1999 • FOUND **North America: USA** • LENGTH *c.*5 m (16 ft) • WEIGHT 1 t
• FOOD **Plants** • YOUNG **Eggs** • LIVED **Early Cretaceous 130–125 million years ago**

Many interesting and rather strange things have been written about this armoured dinosaur. When, in 1999, it was first described to a room full of scientists, they were encouraged to think of it 'as a horny toad blown up to 17 feet long'. They were also told that 'he had shoulder spikes that resemble thorns on a rose but are over a foot long. On both sides of the tail and neck, it had rows of big plates that looked like the triangular dorsal fin on a great white shark. The tail could whip around and cut you bad.' The speakers were Don Burge and James Kirkland .

Gastonia was found in the same quarry as *Utahraptor* (see page 75). It is unlikely that this agile predator would have sought out a 1-tonne armoured dinosaur for a meal, but numerous raptors in a group attack may have succeeded in killing a very young *Gastonia*.

Cerapods

Hylaeosaurus hi-lee-oh-saw-rus
Woodland Lizard

Ornithischia • Genasauria • Thyreophoroidea • Eurypoda • Ankylosauria • Family: Ankylosauridae

FIRST DESCRIBED 1833 • FOUND **Europe: England** • LENGTH **c.6 m (20 ft)** • WEIGHT **2 t** • FOOD **Plants** • YOUNG **Eggs** • LIVED **Early Cretaceous 140–125 million years ago**

Hylaeosaurus was one of the original reptiles that Sir Richard Owen used to define his group, the Dinosauria or dinosaurs. It was first described by Gideon Mantell in 1833. Up to this time, only the front end of the body has been found, and the description of this large relative of *Polacanthus* is based on an incomplete skeleton found near East Grinstead in the south-east of England. *Hylaeosaurus* had a low, heavily built body which was almost completely covered by bony plates and spines. The neck region was armoured by three rows of oval plates and an apron of long spines that pointed out and away from the body, protecting the shoulders and hips. It is thought that there were also some vertical spines over the neck area. There were two rows of slightly backward-pointing spines over the hip region and along the tail. The head was rather flat and long, and similar to that of the modern Komodo dragon.

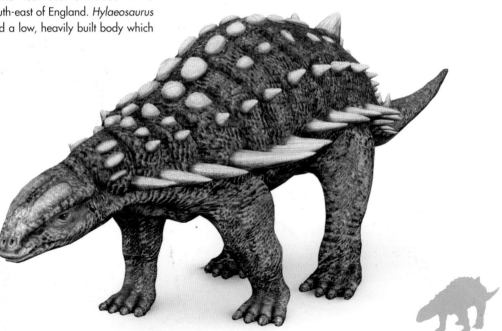

Sauropelta saw-roe-pel-ta

Lizard Shield

Ornithischia • Genasauria • Thyreophoroidea • Eurypoda • Ankylosauria
• Family: Nodosauridae

FIRST DESCRIBED 1970 • FOUND North America: USA • LENGTH c.8 m (26 ft) • WEIGHT 3.5 t
• FOOD Plants • YOUNG Eggs • LIVED Early Cretaceous 125–100 million years ago

Sauropelta lived in the western area of North America during the Early Cretaceous period. At that time, the climate was rather similar to today, with ice and snow present in the polar regions. A large inland sea covered a huge area east of the Rocky Mountains, and coal-forming swamps bordered forested areas. Flowering plants were becoming common and the region supported great herds of bird-hipped dinosaurs. Like many other armoured dinosaurs, *Sauropelta* found these conditions ideal.

It was a truly massive creature which walked on all fours with its belly close to the ground. The back legs were quite a lot longer than the front limbs, and the tail was roughly the same length as the body. As the name suggests, 'Lizard Shield' had a full cover of armour over its back and tail, and the plates that protected the neck were especially spiny. Weighing in at roughly the same weight as a major predator, a fully grown *Sauropelta* would have been a very difficult target for even the most aggressive meat eater.

Cerapods

Ankylosaurus An-ky-low-saw-rus
Stiff Lizard

Ornithischia • Genasauria • Thyreophoroidea • Eurypoda • Ankylosauria
• Family: Ankylosauridae

First Described **1908** • Found **North America: USA, Canada; ?South America** • Length **c.10 m (33 ft)** •
Weight **7 t** • Food **Plants** • Young **Eggs** • Lived **Early Cretaceous 68–65 million years ago**

Ankylosaurus was a truly massive dinosaur. It was the largest ankylosaur, with some scientists suggesting that there may have been giants of 15–17 m (50–56 ft) long. These would have weighed over ten tonnes, and it is extremely unlikely that even *Tyrannosaurus rex* (see page 64) would have tried to kill a healthy animal. Adults had skulls over 1 m (3 ft) in length. The skull was broad with a very thick roof and four triangular horns on the back corners. The snout was beak-like and the animal fed by snipping or cutting plant material, which was then finely ground by the small teeth that covered the palate. Bony shields which fitted into one another covered the neck and body of this slow-moving titan, and there was a huge club at the tip of the tail. The club was made up of two heavily thickened bones, one on either side of the tail. Though they were very heavy, the tail and the club were held high off the ground. If attacked, *Ankylosaurus* would try to move into a position where it could land heavy blows on the legs or soft underbelly of the attacker.

Edmontonia ed-mon-toh-nee-ah

Out of Edmonton

Ornithischia • Genasauria • Thyreophoroidea • Eurypoda • Ankylosauria
• Family: Nodosauridae

FIRST DISCOVERED **1924** • FOUND **North America: Canada, USA** • LENGTH *c.***7 m (23 ft)** • WEIGHT **4 t**
• FOOD **Plants** • YOUNG **Eggs** • LIVED **Early Cretaceous 78–68 million years ago**

Edmontonia is one of the largest armoured dinosaurs on record. Approximately eight complete, or nearly complete, skeletons have been found. *Edmontonia* was first discovered in 1924 in the dinosaur bone beds around Drumheller, Alberta, western Canada. Since then, other remains have been dug up in Montana, South Dakota and Texas.

There are several different kinds of *Edmontonia*. They are identified by the length of the shoulder spikes and what kind of body armour they have. The best-known form is *Edmontonia longiceps* or 'the dinosaur with long spines from Edmonton'.

Edmontonia's head was rather box-like. The beak seems to have had a rounded shape, and there were several rows of small teeth lining the edges of the jaws. The huge shoulder spikes could be used effectively as horns against a hungry predator. Rows of bony shields across the neck and more rows of bony plates along the back and tail gave *Edmontonia* quite a lot of protection. Strangely, it had a very long tail.

Ankylosaurs

Euoplocephalus you-oh-plo-seph-ah-lus
Well-armoured Head

Ornithischia • Genasauria • Thyreophoroidea • Eurypoda • Ankylosauria
• Family: Ankylosauridae

FIRST DESCRIBED **1910** • FOUND **North America: Canada, USA** • LENGTH **c.6 m (20 ft)** • WEIGHT **2.5 t**
• FOOD **Plants** • YOUNG **Eggs** • LIVED **Late Cretaceous 78–68 million years ago**

Ankylosaurs

'Reptilian tanks' were commonplace during the Late Cretaceous, between 70 and 65 million years ago. Herds of Ornithischians with protective body armour dominated the open lands of North America. Their protective armour greatly increased their chances of a long life. *Euoplocephalus* was particularly suited to the time and environment. Its armour covered almost the whole of its body, from the tip of its nose to the end of its tail.

Euoplocephalus, and its close relatives may have had a particularly good sense of smell which would have helped it to find food, avoid enemies and seek out a mate. Its head was more rounded than that of *Ankylosaurus* (see page 96), with a broader beak and teeth in the palate (roof of the mouth). *Euoplocephalus* probably fed on a wide variety of plant material.

Apart from its 'suit of mail', *Euoplocephalus* was blessed with sturdy spines on the back of its head and rows of plates and spikes along its back. The last part of its tail was stiffened by a sheath of bony rods and tipped by a huge, bony, mace-like ball. The animal could use its tail as a club to protect it from predators or during fights with other dominant males.

Huayangosaurus wah-yang-go-saw-rus

Huayang Lizard

Ornithischia • Genasauria • Thyreophoroidea • Eurypoda • Stegosauria
• Family: Huayangosauridae

FIRST DESCRIBED **1982** • FOUND **Asia: China** • LENGTH **c.4 m (13 ft)** • WEIGHT **450 kg (990 lb)** • FOOD **Plants**
• YOUNG **Eggs** • LIVED **Middle Jurassic 166–162 million years ago**

Huayangosaurus is an early, rather primitive relative of *Stegosaurus* (see page 101). In life it would have looked similar to *Stegosaurus*, with two rows of vertical plates running along the top of its body. The two rows began just behind the head and the tallest and largest plates were over the back of the animal. There were huge spikes on its shoulders and at the end of its long tail. Stegosaurs can also be described as armoured dinosaurs, but they were generally much lighter and more agile. They were small to medium in size and had fairly small brains.

Huayangosaurus was quite big, with a rather deep, square-shaped skull. Unlike *Stegosaurus*, the 'Huayang Lizard' still had teeth at the front of its jaw. It held its body high off the ground on heavily built limbs and feet like those of a modern elephant. The front feet had five very short toes, whereas the back feet had only three, though they were bigger and far more robust. All stegosaurs were plant eaters.

Stegosaurs

Kentrosaurus ken-tro-saw-rus

Spiky Lizard

Ornithischia • Genasauria • Thyreophoroidea • Eurypoda • Stegosauria
• Family: Stegosauridae

First Described **1915** • Found **Africa** • Length **c.4 m (13 ft)** • Weight **450 kg (990 lb)** • Food **Plants**
• Young **Eggs** • Lived **Late Jurassic 154–151 million years ago**

Stegosaurs

Kentrosaurus is closely related to *Stegosaurus* (see page 101) but it is smaller, and the paired plates along its back give way to pairs of tall spines over the hips and long tail. This is why it is called the 'Spiky Lizard'.

Kentrosaurus was found in 1909, in Tanzania, by a German expedition. Hundreds of bones of about 70 individuals were recovered. From these bones the scientists could build two complete skeletons. Sadly, one of them was completely destroyed when a bomb hit the Humboldt Museum in Berlin, during the Second World War.

Like *Stegosaurus*, *Kentrosaurus* had a long, narrow head. It had a horny beak for cutting and slicing plant material and many small teeth, behind the beak, for more crushing and grinding. The huge number of bones found during the original expedition suggests that *Kentrosaurus* lived in herds near lakes and rivers. They lived at the same time as the *Elaphrosaurus* ('Lightweight Lizard') and several meat eaters. These may have been *Kentrosaurus*'s natural enemies, but it is most likely that 70 individuals died as a result of some natural disaster such as a flood.

Stegosaurus steg-oh-saw-rus

Roofed Lizard

Ornithischia • Genasauria • Thyreophoroidea • Eurypoda • Stegosauria
• Family: Stegosauridae

FIRST DESCRIBED 1877 • FOUND **North America: USA; ?Africa: Madagascar** • LENGTH *c.*9 m (30 ft)
• WEIGHT **2.5 t** • FOOD **Plants** • YOUNG **Eggs** • LIVED **Late Jurassic 154–146 million years ago**

If there was a prize for the most famous dinosaur, then *Stegosaurus* and *Tyrannosaurus* (see page 64) would be the two main contenders. They are totally different animals but both have excited our imaginations. *Stegosaurus* was a placid plant eater with an exceptionally small brain. It had a long, flattened head with a beaked mouth. The jaw teeth were small and probably rubbed against one another like grindstones as the animal chewed its food before swallowing. *Stegosaurus* was the largest of the stegosaur dinosaurs. It is easily recognized by the two rows of vertical plates along its back and the four huge spikes on its tail.

What could *Stegosaurus*'s plates have been for? They are slightly off-set and inside there are recognizable channels that probably filled with blood. They may have acted like radiators. Alternatively, they may have been used for display between males and females. They would not have been much use for protecting the animal during an attack. For this, *Stegosaurus* relied on its four-spiked tail. Each spike was about 1 m long (3 ft) , and could have inflicted terrible wounds on the legs and underbelly of its tormentor.

Stegosaurs

Dacentrurus dah-sen-troo-russ

Pointed Tail

Ornithischia • Genasauria • Thyreophoroidea • Eurypoda • Stegosauria
• Family: Stegosauridae

FIRST DESCRIBED 1902 • FOUND **Europe: England, France, Portugal** • LENGTH *c*.6 m (20 ft) • WEIGHT **2 t**
• FOOD **Plants** • YOUNG **Eggs** • LIVED **Late Jurassic 160–150 million years ago**

Stegosaurs

Dacentrurus was the first from the stegosaur family to be described from the fossil record. In 1875 Sir Richard Owen first said that these bones belonged to *Omosaurus*, but that name had already been used for another animal. In 1902 the palaeontologist Frederic Lucas introduced the name we use today. *Dacentrurus* seems to have lived throughout Western Europe, though most remains have been found in southern England.

Scientists have argued fiercely about the size of this animal. Some have suggested that individuals may have reached 10 m (33 ft) in length and weighed in at as much as 6 tonnes. *Dacentrurus* had long front limbs and spines, rather than plates, along the length of its back. It is thought, therefore, to have been a primitive stegosaur. No skull remains have been found from the various parts of Europe where *Dacentrurus* is known to have lived. It is assumed that the skull was quite small and housed a tiny brain. The size of the legs suggests that it was a heavily built stegosaur that 'grazed' on quite soft plant material.

Hypsilophodon hip-see-loaf-oh-don

High-ridged Tooth

Ornithischia • Genasauria • Cerapoda • Ornithopoda • Family: Hypsilophodontidae

FIRST DISCOVERED **1849** • FOUND **Worldwide: Europe; North America; Asia** • LENGTH **c.2.5 m (8 ft)**
• WEIGHT **25 kg (55 lb)** • FOOD **Plants** • YOUNG **Eggs** • LIVED **Early Cretaceous 130–115 million years ago**

Although the remains of *Hypsilophodon* were discovered in 1849, the animal was not named until 1889. The reason for the delay was simple: 19th-century scientists thought it was a baby *Iguanodon* (see page 106). For the next 80 years this tiny ornithopod (bird-footed dinosaur) was thought to be a tree dweller. In fact, a model of *Hypsilophodon* holding on to a branch was a central exhibit at the Natural History Museum in London for many years.

More recently, however, experts have worked out that this was an agile little dinosaur with long, strongly built back legs and short arms. It had quite a large head with a beak at the front of its mouth and a row of small grinding teeth behind. As its name suggests, these teeth were ridged. *Hypsilophodon* was a founder member of the *Iguanodon* line of dinosaurs, which reached its peak with the appearance of the duck-billed dinosaurs during the Cretaceous. It may have evolved from an animal such as *Heterodontosaurus*. The *Hypsilophodon* was a primitive ornithopod from the Early Cretaceous.

Ornithopods

Leaellynasaura lay-ell-lye-nuh-saw-rah

Leaellyn's Lizard

Ornithischia • Genasauria • Cerapoda • Ornithopoda • Euornithopoda
• Family: Hypsilophodontidae

FIRST DESCRIBED 1989 • FOUND Australasia: Australia • LENGTH c.1.5 m (5 ft) • WEIGHT 40 kg (90 lb)
• FOOD Plants • YOUNG Eggs • LIVED Early Cretaceous 125–100 million years ago

During the late 1970s, scientists found hundreds of dinosaur bones in a site now known as Dinosaur Cove in southeastern Australia. They were from many separate animals, but with careful preparation and reconstruction, the scientists were able to reassemble the skeleton of a small to medium-sized dinosaur. One of the finest fossils was the tiny skull of a baby dinosaur. This juvenile was less than 75 cm (2½ ft) long and only 800 g (1 lb 10 oz) in weight. The scientists, Tom and Patricia Rich, decided to name the baby after their own daughter, Leaellyn.

Brain casts from other remains suggest that *Leaellynasaura* had large eyes and keen eyesight. It was very agile and may have been covered in a 'furry' or down-like coat. During the Early Cretaceous, Australia was near to the southern polar ice cap. The seasons were very marked but it seems that 'Leaellyn's Lizard' was well able to survive the harsh conditions of the dark winter months.

Dryosaurus dry-oh-saw-rus

Oak Lizard

Ornithischia • Genasauria • Cerapoda • Ornithopoda • Dryomorpha
• Family: Dryosauridae

FIRST DESCRIBED 1894 • FOUND North America: USA; Africa: Tanzania • LENGTH c.3 m (10 ft)
• WEIGHT 80 kg (175 lb) • FOOD Plants • YOUNG Eggs • LIVED Late Jurassic 154–146 million years ago

Apart from being a lot bigger, the 'Oak Lizard' was quite similar to *Hypsilophodon* (see page 103) in overall appearance. It was two-legged with short arms and is best described as lightly built and agile. The head was quite deep, with sharp, deeply ridged teeth like those of its distant cousin. According to some scientists, *Dryosaurus* is the last ornithopod to have had short arms.

Like the *Hypsilophodon* and *Leaellynasaura* (see page 104), *Dryosaurus* had large eyes and was probably quite intelligent. It lived in groups or small herds and used its keen eyesight and speed to avoid being caught and eaten. Adult specimens may have reached 4 m (13 ft) in length. *Dryosaurus* had a relatively long neck and slim body balanced by a long, stiffened tail.

It may seem strange that an animal is known from fossils found in two countries that are now separated by thousand of miles of land and sea. During the Late Jurassic, however, the American and African continents were joined together, and it was possible for even the smallest dinosaurs to exist over a large area during a million years or so of Earth's history.

Ornithopods

Iguanodon ig-wan-oh-don

Iguana Tooth

Ornithischia • Genasauria • Cerapoda • Ornithopoda • Family: Iguanodontidae

FIRST DISCOVERED **1809** • FOUND **Europe; North America; ?Africa; Asia** • LENGTH **c.10 m (33 ft)** • WEIGHT **5 t** • FOOD **Plants** • YOUNG **Eggs** • LIVED **Late Jurassic–Early Cretaceous 150–126 million years ago**

Iguanodon, *Megalosaurus* (see page 51) and *Hylaeosaurus* (see page 94) were the first three animals to be called dinosaurs – Dinosauria. Since it was first found and described in southeast England, in 1825, *Iguanodon* has been found in many areas of the world. At first, scientists thought that this large ornithopod walked on all fours and that the head had a horn over the nose. It is now known that it probably spent most of its time on two legs and that the 'horn' was actually a spike on the end of its thumb.

Many skeletons have been found throughout Europe, including, in 1878, 24 beautiful specimens from Belgium. These skeletons are now on display in the Royal Belgian Institute of Natural Sciences in Brussels. This wonderful discovery suggests that *Iguanodon* was a herd animal and that adults and young would roam together along river banks and lakesides in search of food.

Iguanodon had a large head with a long, forward-sloping snout, a horny beak and many leaf-shaped teeth set into the jawbones. This dinosaur could chew its food and so break down quite tough plant matter. The origins of the hadrosaurs (duck-billed dinosaurs) can be traced back to *Iguanodon*.

Camptosaurus kamp-toe-saw-rus

Flexible Lizard

Ornithischia • Genasauria • Cerapoda • Ornithopoda • Family: Camptosauridae

FIRST DESCRIBED 1885 • FOUND North America, Western USA; Europe • LENGTH *c.*7 m (23 ft) • WEIGHT 1 t
• FOOD Plants • YOUNG Eggs • LIVED Late Jurassic–?Early Cretaceous 154–126 million years ago

Camptosaurus looked very much like a smaller *Iguanodon*. It had a fairly large head, a short neck and a long tail. The arms were quite long with four fingers and a sharp spur for a thumb. It had long, strongly built hind limbs with broad feet. Most of the bone remains that have been used to describe this dinosaur come from the American species, *Camptosaurus dispar*, from Colorado, Oklahoma, Utah and Wyoming. Adult and young (juvenile) skeletons have been unearthed.

Like *Iguanodon*, the 'Flexible Lizard' was an efficient plant eater. It had a long, horse-like muzzle and a horned beak. There were two rows of leaf-like, ridged teeth on both the upper and lower jaws. These rows were slightly offset to form a chewing and grinding surface for food.

They worked in much the same way as the sets of teeth found in the hadrosaurs (duck-billed) dinosaurs.

Camptosaurus probably relied on speed alone to avoid attack from its enemies. It is likely that it could outrun large meat eaters. The long tail would have given the animal perfect balance as it leaned slightly forward to gain and maintain speed.

Iguanodontids

Ouranosaurus oo-ran-oh-saw-rus

Brave Lizard

Ornithischia • Genasauria • Cerapoda • Ornithopoda • Family: Iguanodontidae

FIRST DESCRIBED **1976** • FOUND **Africa: Niger** • LENGTH **c.7 m (23 ft)** • WEIGHT **4 t** • FOOD **Plants**
• YOUNG **Eggs** • LIVED **Early Cretaceous 125–112 million years ago**

Iguanodontids

The barren, desert landscape of what is now the African state of Niger seems an unlikely place to find dinosaurs. About 120 million years ago, however, it would have looked very different, with lakes and swamps bordered by huge forests. These wetlands were ideal for the preservation of fossils, and carcasses of dead dinosaurs and trunks of giant trees were quickly preserved in the fine black muds that accumulated there over the ages.

Ouranosaurus was similar to *Iguanodon* (see page 106) but had a sail along its back. The sail was made of skin drawn tightly over tall spines that rose up from the backbone. It was probably used to control body temperature: it provided a large surface area which allowed cool air to draw heat from the many blood vessels that ran through the skin.

Ouranosaurus had a large head with a long snout. The mouth had a horny beak at the front, and many big teeth lined the long upper and lower jaws. Both *Iguanodon* and *Ouranosaurus* had long tongues that could be used to gather food.

Tenontosaurus ten-on-toe-saw-rus

Tendon Lizard

Ornithischia • Genasauria • Cerapoda • Ornithopoda • Family: ?Iguanodontidae

FIRST DESCRIBED 1970 • FOUND North America: USA • LENGTH c.6.5 m (21 ft) • WEIGHT 1 t
• FOOD Plants • YOUNG Eggs • LIVED Early Cretaceous 122–110 million years ago

Tenontosaurus was a rather distant relative of Iguanodon (see page 106), and scientists are still reluctant to link the two within the same family. In some ways they were similar, but Tenontosaurus had quite long, heavy front legs, a rather short neck and a very long tail. It also had a very stiff lower back and hip area because of massively developed tendons (fibres which connect muscle to bone), bundles of which ran alongside the backbone. Sometimes the softer tendons were turned to bone (ossified) to give even greater stiffness.

Tenontosaurus probably spent much of its life on all fours. Its tail was raised high off the ground, and the 'Tendon Lizard' most likely fed on shrubs and bushes rather than from the higher branches of tall trees. Like Iguanodon it had a beaked mouth and a limited number of jaw teeth. Interestingly, Deinonychus (see page 73) teeth have been found with the skeletons of this rather slow-moving, plant eater. Perhaps, in this instance, Tenontosaurus had met a sad end at the jaws of this vicious killer.

Iguanodontids

Bactrosaurus back-troh- saw-rus

Club-spined Lizard

Ornithischia • Genasauria • Cerapoda • Ornithopoda • Iguanodontia
• Family: ?Hadrosauridae

FIRST DESCRIBED **1933** • FOUND **Asia: Mongolia, ?Russia** • LENGTH **c.6 m (20 ft)** • WEIGHT **1.5 t** • FOOD **Plants**
• YOUNG **Eggs** • LIVED **Late Cretaceous 78–68 million years ago**

The first bones of *Bactrosaurus* were found in Mongolia in the early 1930s. There are now six complete skeletons known to science, and there may also have been remains found in Russia.

Bactrosaurus is one of the first duck-billed dinosaurs or hadrosaurs to have appeared on Earth. It was quite small but had many of the features of later, much larger creatures. *Bactrosaurus*'s head was fairly large and quite deep and there were traces of a bump or swelling over the nose. This suggests that it was more closely related to the crested duckbills, such as *Lambeosaurus* (see page 113), than to those without crests, such as *Edmontosaurus* (see page 111) and *Hadrosaurus*. But like the crested and the non-crested duckbills, *Bactrosaurus* had a huge number of teeth in its upper and lower jaws. These fitted tightly together to form a flat grinding surface. This arrangement of the teeth is known as a 'battery'.

Bactrosaurus was a heavily built, two-legged, plant eater with fairly short arms. All duck-billed dinosaurs had hoof-like toes, so that they could run quickly over firm ground to avoid being cornered by a huge meat eater such as *Tarbosaurus* (see page 63).

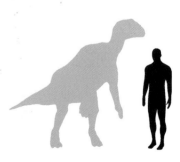

Edmontosaurus ed-mont-oh-saw-rus

Edmonton Lizard

Ornithischia • Genasauria • Cerapoda • Ornithopoda • Iguanodontia
• Family: Hadrosauridae

FIRST DESCRIBED 1917 • FOUND **North America: Canada, USA** • LENGTH **c.13 m (43 ft)** • WEIGHT **3 t**
• FOOD **Plants** • YOUNG **Eggs** • LIVED **Late Cretaceous 70–66 million years ago**

Edmontosaurus may have been the biggest of the duck-billed dinosaurs (hadrosaurs). It was a flat-headed or non-crested type that closely resembled its ancestors, the iguanodontids.

Bactrosaurus (see page 110) seems to have been the link between the two families. The hadrosaurs are thought to have been the last of the major groups of dinosaurs to appear in the fossil record. But, during the final episode of the Late Cretaceous, they evolved in spectacular fashion to give rise to the flat-headed and crested forms.

Edmontosaurus was a herding animal that lived during Late Cretaceous times around an inland sea in what is now western North America. The climate varied with the seasons but basically it was warm and quite wet. Huge forests bordered the wetland areas and broad open plains supported many herds of ornithopod dinosaurs.

Edmontosaurus's head was large and had a flattened, duck-billed snout. There were nearly a thousand teeth in the upper and lower jaws. They were arranged in batteries (flattened rows) that formed a crushing surface similar to that of the huge cheek teeth of a modern elephant. A long tongue helped the animal gather its food.

Hadrosaurs

Corythosaurus kor-ryth-oh-saw-rus

Corinthian Crested Lizard

Ornithischia • Genasauria • Cerapoda • Ornithopoda • Iguanodontia
• Family: Hadrosauridae

FIRST DESCRIBED **1914** • FOUND **North America: Canada, USA** • LENGTH **c.10 m (33 ft)** • WEIGHT **4 t**
• FOOD **Plants** • YOUNG **Eggs** • LIVED **Late Cretaceous 83–71 million years ago**

Crested Hadrosaurs

Corythosaurus is a large, crested hadrosaur (duck-billed) dinosaur. It is closely related to animals like *Saurolophus* and *Parasaurolophus* (see page 114). The bodies of these creatures were rather similar in shape to those of *Iguanodon* (see page 106) or *Edmontosaurus* (a hadrosaur without a crest, see page 111), with the three toes on the hind limbs being hoof-like. It seems likely that *Iguanodon* was the ancestor of all duckbills.

Many skulls of *Corythosaurus* have been found in Montana in the western United States and in Alberta, Canada, The skulls vary in size and include numbers of adult males, females and juveniles. The most obvious differences between the sexes and between young and old are the size and shape of the crest. The crest probably helped animals of all ages to identify one another as well as their own herd during feeding and migration. The name 'Corinthian Crested Lizard' comes from the shape of the helmets worn by the soldiers of the ancient Greek city of Corinth in about 800BC.

Lambeosaurus lam-bee-oh-saw-rus

Lambe's Lizard

Ornithischia • Genasauria • Cerapoda • Ornithopoda • Iguanodontia • Family: Lambeosauridae

FIRST DESCRIBED 1923 • FOUND **North and Central America: Canada, USA, ?Mexico** • LENGTH ***c*.13 m (43 ft)** • WEIGHT **4 t** • FOOD **Plants** • YOUNG **Eggs** • LIVED **Late Cretaceous 82–72 million years ago**

Lambeosaurus was a huge, duck-billed dinosaur. It was almost twice the size of *Bactrosaurus* (see page 110), from which it may have evolved. 'Lambe's Lizard' was about the same size as *Edmontosaurus* (see page 111) but was instantly recog-nizable because of the large crest at the top of the skull. In males, the crest was two-pronged whereas that of the female and juveniles was smaller and only single. The male crest has

been described as 'hatchet-like'. Hadrosaur crests were used for display and recognition although some scientists believe that they contained salt glands. Some have suggested that *Parasaurolophus*'s crest (see page 114) could have been used as a kind of amplifier for loud calling or as a snorkel for swimming underwater, but this latter idea has now been abandoned. Nile crocodiles are known to roar or call out and it is likely that male hadrosaurs could roar or bellow during mating or when there was danger about.

Adult duck-billed hadrosaurs, such as the males of *Lambeosaurus*, probably spent most of their life on all fours, collecting and grinding quite tough plant material for food.

Parasaurolophus par-ah-saw-roh-loaf-us
Side-ridge Lizard

Ornithischia • Genasauria • Cerapoda • Ornithopoda • Iguanodontia
• Family: Lambeosauridae

FIRST DESCRIBED **1922** • FOUND **North America: Canada, USA** • LENGTH *c.*10 m (33 ft)
• WEIGHT **3 t** • FOOD **Plants** • YOUNG **Eggs** • LIVED **Late Cretaceous 82–66 million years ago**

Parasaurolophus was first discovered in 1921 during one of the great expeditions to the Canadian badland area of Alberta. Here, the Red Deer River has cut hundreds of small valleys down into the local rocks to dramatic effect. The region was difficult to cross by foot or on horses, so that the dinosaur explorers usually travelled by river. Today travel there is much easier and thousands of visitors can go to the Tyrell Museum in Drumheller and take part in organized digs.

Beautiful displays of over 30 types of dinosaurs include superb skeletons of *Parasaurolophus*. Though not as big as *Lambeosaurus* (see page 113), the 'Side-ridged Lizard'

has a spectacular, curved crest that stretches up and over the snout for almost 2 m (6½ ft). There are no holes in the crest and the old idea that it might have served as a snorkel underwater has now been abandoned. Instead, the tubular crest may have amplified

the sound as groups of dinosaurs called to one another while they were feeding in wooded areas.

Archaeopteryx ark-ee-op-ter-icks

Ancient Feather

Aves or Theropoda • Tetanurae • Coelurosauria • Family: Archaeopteridae

FIRST DESCRIBED **1861** • FOUND **Europe: Germany** • LENGTH **c.45 m (18 in)** • WEIGHT **500 g (1 lb 2 oz)** • FOOD **Insects, worms** • YOUNG **Eggs** • LIVED **Late Jurassic 148–146 million years ago**

'Is it a bird or is it a dinosaur?' This is the question that has puzzled scientists since 'Archie' was first discovered in the 1860s. The first six fossils, found in the lithographic stone (print stone) quarries of southern Germany, showed the delicate impressions of feathers. For over a hundred years scientists believed that because *Archaeopteryx* had feathers it could not be a dinosaur. Arguments raged over the origins of the first bird, however, and whether or not the evolution of feathers was linked with flight. But now we have unearthed many feathered dinosaurs and we are concerned more with which dinosaur family is directly linked with the evolution of *Archaeopteryx*.

'Archie' had many sharp teeth and there were two well-developed fingers on the front edge of the wings. These are primitive characteritics and, in many ways, *Archaeopteryx* seemed more closely related to the tiny theropod *Compsognathus* (see page 58) than to modern-day birds. But, wings, feathers and lightweight hollow bones are typical of birds. This means that *Archaeopteryx* is a truly unique animal that bridges the gap between dinosaurs, such as *Coelurosaurus* and *Compsognathus* and their descendants: gulls, herons and pigeons.

Birds

Confuciusornis con-few-shus-orn-iss

Wing without Tooth

Aviale (Aves) • Confuciusornithiformes

First Described **1996** • Found **Asia: China** • Length **c.20 cm (8 in)** • Weight **150 g (5 oz)**
• Food **Seeds, insects** • Young **Eggs** • Lived **Early Cretaceous 130–125 million years ago**

Birds

Hundreds of skeletons of this small bird have been found in China. Many bear the impressions of feathers as well as bones. There are males and females and, as with dinosaurs, the male birds are larger. *Confuciusornis* was the first bird with a proper bill (beak). It appeared between 10 and 12 million years after *Archaeopteryx* (see page 115).

Scientists have been able to reconstruct full-scale models of this bird and the final result is about the size of a crow. Most are brightly coloured, with green, red and yellow plumage. The tail feathers are very long, especially in the males. It is thought that *Confuciusornis* was a tree dweller and that hundreds, perhaps even thousands, of birds flocked together in woodland areas.

As well as a bill, *Confuciusornis* had a well-developed breastplate, or sternum, which had a mid-line crest to which muscles could be attached. In *Archaeopteryx* the breastplate was poorly developed and prolonged flight would have almost certainly been impossible. *Confuciusornis* may be a direct ancestor of modern birds.

Ichthyornis ick-thee-orn-iss

Fish Bird

Aviale (Aves) • Ondotoholcae (Cretaceous toothed birds) Icthyornithiformes

FIRST DESCRIBED **1872** • FOUND **North America: USA, Canada** • LENGTH **c.3 m (12 in)**
• WEIGHT **300 g (10 oz)** • FOOD **Fish** • YOUNG **Eggs** • LIVED **Late Cretaceous 100–80 million years ago**

Bones of *Ichthyornis* have been found in Kansas and in Canada. It was a small seabird that lived near the coast of the inland sea that existed in the western part of North America during Late Cretaceous times. Chalk was the main rock type laid down in the seas of this period, and the very first skeleton of *Ichthyornis* was found in the Smoky Hill chalk (North Fork, Kansas).

The remains of this toothed seabird were very delicate but they were beautifully preserved and showed that *Ichthyornis* had upwards of 20 sharp teeth on each side of its lower jaw. There were also teeth towards the back of the upper jaw. Both sets curved slightly backwards, an important clue to the way in which *Ichthyornis* fed. Backward-facing teeth allow animals to hang on to their prey without fear of losing it. *Ichthyornis* probably scooped up fish on the surface of the sea, but it may also have dived in much the same way as a gannet does today.

Birds

Hesperornis hess-per-orn-iss
Western Bird

Aviale (Aves) • Ondotoholcae (Cretaceous toothed birds) • Hesperornithiformes

FIRST DESCRIBED 1872 • FOUND North America: USA • HEIGHT c.2 m (6½ ft) • WEIGHT 25 kg (55 lb)
• FOOD Fish • YOUNG Eggs • LIVED Late Cretaceous 82–76 million years ago

Birds

As well as the remains of *Ichthyornis* (see page 117), the Smoky Hill chalk of Kansas in the United States contained the remains of another toothed bird. *Hesperornis* was, however, a flightless giant with tiny wings, a large body and strange legs. It is odd that these birds should adopt such a lifestyle, but it seems to have hopped around on land and dived into the sea in search of food. *Hesperornis* was, in effect, a giant version of today's 'grebe' and is known only from the northern hemisphere of the Cretaceous world.

It had a long beak with many teeth which were arranged in a similar way to those of *Ichthyornis*. The 'Western Bird' had a very short thigh bone, and the longer lower limbs and paddle-like feet extended sideways away from the body. On land, this heavily built bird would have walked with an ungainly waddle but in the sea it became a powerful and graceful swimmer. *Hesperornis* fed on the abundance of small fish that flourished in the warm Cretaceous seas.

Diatryma dye-ah-try-mah

Terror Crane

Aviale (Aves) • Neornithes (Modern Birds) • Diatrymiformes

FIRST DESCRIBED 1876 • FOUND **North America: USA; Europe: France, Germany**
• HEIGHT **c.3 m (10 ft)** • WEIGHT **150 kg (330 lb)** • FOOD **Meat, plants** • YOUNG **Eggs**
• LIVED **Palaeocene–Middle Eocene 65–48 million years ago**

When the dinosaurs became extinct, other animals took advantage of the new opportunities for feeding that opened up at the beginning of the Age of Mammals, 65 million years ago. Birds were some of the first to benefit from the new world order, particularly these giant Terror Cranes. For many years it was assumed that these huge creatures, with their massive heads and vicious bills, took over the role of their distant cousins, the medium-sized, meat-eating dinosaurs.

Some 80 per cent of modern birds are supposed to have evolved during the Palaeocene–Eocene period, and *Diatryma* was one of the first. It was a flightless bird similar in form to an ostrich or a Moa, but was probably much heavier than either. It may have trapped and killed small to medium-sized mammals for food. *Diatryma* was a fast runner and, once it had caught its victim, could hold it on the ground with its large clawed feet. One savage blow with its enormous beak would have been enough to still its prey. Recently, some scientists have argued that *Diatryma* was not a meat eater at all, but this is still to be proved.

Birds

Peteinosaurus pet-ine-oh-saw-rus
Winged Lizard

Pterosauria • Rhamphorynchoidea • Family: Dimorphodontidae

FIRST DESCRIBED **1978** • FOUND **Europe: Italy** • WINGSPAN **c.60 cm (2 ft)** • WEIGHT **200 g (7 oz)** • FOOD **Insects**
• YOUNG **Eggs** • LIVED **Triassic 215–204 million years ago**

Pterosaurs

Dinosaurs did not fly. During the Age of the Dinosaurs (230–65 million years ago), the skies were ruled by pterosaurs, a group of flying reptiles. They were distant relatives of the dinosaurs, crocodiles, snakes and lizards, which all belong to the same group.

Pterosaur wingspans ranged from tens of centimetres to tens of metres. Each wing was made up of a sheet of skin stretched between a long finger on the hand to the outer edge of the foot. *Peteinosaurus* was fairly small with a 60-cm (2-ft) wingspan. It had a fairly large head with many sharp, pointed teeth. The front teeth were like long fangs, while the cheek teeth were flattened sideways and had sharp cutting edges to the front and back. This type of tooth is thought to be typical of primitive, early pterosaurs. The 'Winged Lizard' had a long tail which was vitally important during flight, acting as a rudder as the animal swooped and dived in search of flying insects, its main food.

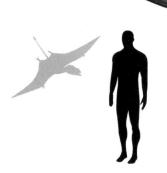

Eudimorphodon eu-dee-morph-oh-don

Two-form Tooth

Pterosauria • Rhamphorynchoidea • Family: Eudimorphododontidae

FIRST DESCRIBED **1973** • FOUND **Europe: Italy** • WINGSPAN **c.1 m (3 ft)** • WEIGHT **2 kg (4.4 lb)**
• FOOD **Fish** • YOUNG **Eggs** • LIVED **Triassic 215–204 million years ago**

Eudimorphodon and *Peteinosaurus* (see page 120) were close neighbours: both animals were found in the Triassic rocks of the Cene region of Italy. And both pterosaurs had long tails. *Eudimorphodon* was the larger animal, however, and its teeth were more advanced than those of its distant cousin. The head of this fish-eating flying reptile was 7 cm (3 in) long and the tips of the lower jaw were bent slightly downwards. The front of the mouth was armed with long, pointed teeth. The shape of the jaw and the arrangement of teeth enabled *Eudimorphodon* to snatch fish from the surface of the sea.

Along the sides of each of the upper and lower jaws, *Eudimorphodon* had many smaller teeth. Each tooth was armed with between three and five points. Fossilized stomach contents suggest that these teeth were used to crush the bones and scales of fish. Teeth used like this are often polished and flattened owing to the constant grinding of the tooth surface against the tough scales.

Pterosaurs

Rhamphorhynchus ram-foh-rink-uss

Beaked Snout

Pterosauria • Rhamphorynchoidea • Family: Rhamphorhynchidae

FIRST DESCRIBED 1973 • FOUND **Europe: Germany; Africa: Tanzania** • WINGSPAN *c.*1.7 m (5½ ft)
• WEIGHT **4 kg (8½ lb)** • FOOD **Fish** • YOUNG **Eggs** • LIVED **Late Jurassic 164–154 million years ago**

Pterosaurs

Rhamphorhynchus is one of the better-known pterosaurs. It lived at the same time as *Compsognathus* (see page 58) and *Archaeopteryx* (see page 115) in southern Germany and perhaps Tanzania. It was small to medium in size and several types were found around lakes and rivers over 150 million years ago. The larger ones had a wingspan of 1.7 m (5½ ft) but the smallest measured less than 20 cm (8 in).

Rhamphorhynchus's head was long and pointed and there may have been a pouch hanging down in which the animal stored its catch. There were only 20 long, forward-pointing teeth on the upper jaw and even fewer on the lower. *Rhamphorhynchus* had a well-developed breastplate or sternum. This flat, broad bone was ideal for the attachment of powerful muscles. The 'Beaked Snout' pterosaur was a very good flyer and it had a long tail that worked as a rudder.

Large areas of the region where *Rhamphorhynchus* lived were covered with water. The rocks deposited at this time were very fine-grained, and lacked oxygen and bacteria. This allowed dead or dying animals to be buried and preserved in magnificent condition, and the fossilized stomach contents of *Rhamphorhynchus* reveal that it lived on small fish and shrimps.`

Anurognathus an-yoor-og-nayth-us

Without Tail and Jaw

Pterosauria • Rhamphorynchoidea • Family: Anurognathidae

FIRST DESCRIBED **1923** • FOUND **Europe: Germany** • WINGSPAN **c.50 cm (20 in)** • WEIGHT **500 g (1 lb 2 oz)**
• FOOD **Insects** • YOUNG **Eggs** • LIVED **Late Jurassic 164–154 million years ago**

Anurognathus is a very strange relative of *Rhamphorhynchus* (see page 122). Both pterosaurs lived at the same time and both are found in the Solnhofen Limestone of southern Germany. *Anurognathus* is known only from a single skeleton but these scant remains show that it had a very short tail and a rather small but distinctive head. The skull was only 3 cm (1¼ in) long but it had large eyes and a wide mouth with small peg-like teeth.

In contrast to the long-snouted *Rhamphorhynchus*, *Anurognathus* looked more like a midget meat eating dinosaur: the head was much deeper and definitely more rounded. In proportion to the head and body, the wings were long and rather narrow. As in all pterosaurs, a long fourth finger supported the wing. Fingers one, two and three were placed about a third of the way down the leading edge of wing. They were very short and were used mostly for gripping on to trees or rock surfaces and when the animal was on all fours. *Anurognathus* was a good flyer and is thought to have fed on the many insects that thronged around lakes and rivers.

Pterosaurs

Pterodactylus terr-oh-dak-tile-us

Winged Finger

Pterosauria • Pterodactyloidea • Family: Pterodactylidae

FIRST DESCRIBED **1809** • FOUND **Europe: Germany, England; Africa: • Tanzania** • WINGSPAN **c.1 m (3 ft)** • WEIGHT **5 kg (11 lb)** • FOOD **Meat** • YOUNG **Eggs** • LIVED **Late Jurassic 155–146 million years ago**

Pterodactylus was the first pterosaur to be described by scientists. It was found in Germany and was a near neighbour of *Rhamphorhynchus* (see page 122) and *Anurognathus* (see page 123) in southern Germany. Skeletons found in the Solnhofen limestone come in a range of sizes and different ages. The smallest example has a wingspan of only 18 cm (7 in), and the body was tiny, just 2 cm (¾ in) long. This was a recently hatched, baby pterodactyl. Its parents were three or four times as large. The largest type of *Pterodactylus* had a wingspan of 2.5 m (8 ft 2 in).

Pterodactylus was the first known member of a new, more advanced group of pterosaurs. They had different proportions from *Rhamphorhynchus* and its relatives, and always had a very short tail. There are other differences in the skull, neck, hands and feet. The pterodactyl family includes the largest creatures ever to fly – the Cretaceous giants such as *Pteranodon* (see page 128) and *Quetzalcoatlus* (see page 130). These great flying reptiles had wingspans the equal of small aeroplanes. They most probably relied on hot-air currents to keep them aloft whereas *Pterodactylus* was an agile and active flyer.

Tapejara tap-eh-jar-rah

Old Being

Pterosauria • Pterodactyloidea • Family: Tapejaridae

FIRST DESCRIBED **1989** • FOUND **South America: Brazil** • WINGSPAN ***c.*4 m (13 ft)** • WEIGHT **15 kg (33 lb)**
• FOOD **Fish, carrion** • YOUNG **Eggs** • LIVED **Early Cretaceous 111–100 million years ago**

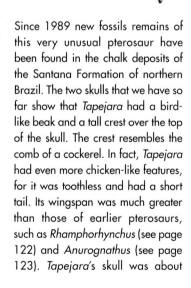

Since 1989 new fossils remains of this very unusual pterosaur have been found in the chalk deposits of the Santana Formation of northern Brazil. The two skulls that we have so far show that *Tapejara* had a bird-like beak and a tall crest over the top of the skull. The crest resembles the comb of a cockerel. In fact, *Tapejara* had even more chicken-like features, for it was toothless and had a short tail. Its wingspan was much greater than those of earlier pterosaurs, such as *Rhamphorhynchus* (see page 122) and *Anurognathus* (see page 123). *Tapejara*'s skull was about

20 cm (8 in) long and, as well as the tall crest towards the back of the head, there was a second, smaller one just over the nose.

Detailed impressions found with the skull suggest that *Tapejara* had a sheet of skin that stretched between these two crests. It is likely that this skin was highly coloured in male animals and that it could be inflated during displays and mating. The end of the lower jaw was rather deep and tipped slightly downwards; this beak-like feature was probably used to catch fish or tear pieces of meat from the carcass of a dead animal.

Pterodactyls

Anhanguera an-han-gwer-ah
Old Devil

Pterosauria • Pterodactyloidea • Family: Anhangueridae

FIRST DESCRIBED **1985** • FOUND **South America: Brazil** • WINGSPAN **c.5.5 m (18 ft)** • WEIGHT **20 kg (44 lb)**
• FOOD **Fish, carrion** • YOUNG **Eggs** • LIVED **Early Cretaceous 111–100 million years ago**

Pterodactyls

Imagine a creature with a 5-m (16-ft) wingspan and a head twice the length of its body. Bizarre to say the least! More than 110 million years ago, however, there was just such a creature, and scientists gave it the apt name of 'Old Devil' or *Anhanguera*, an evil spirit feared by the Tupi Indians of north-eastern Brazil.

Anhanguera was a fish eater and probably caught its food as it flew over the warm inland sea that was present in northern Brazil at that time. *Anhanguera*'s skull was 50 cm (20 in) long and slimly built, rather like that of a pelican. The jaws were deep and there was a distinct crest above the snout. There may have been another smaller crest beneath the lower jaw. Both crests would have helped to hold the head steady during flight. Strangely, the back legs of *Anhanguera* were splayed outwards away from the body and the hips were quite tiny. This means that, when it was on the ground, *Anhanguera* would have had to struggle along on all fours.

Dsungaripterus jung-ah-rip-ter-us
Junggar Basin Wing

Pterosauria • Pterodactyloidea • Family: Dsungaripteridae

FIRST DESCRIBED **1964** • FOUND **Asia: China; Africa: Tanzania** • WINGSPAN **c.3 m (10 ft)** • WEIGHT **20 kg (44 lb)**
• FOOD **Shellfish** • YOUNG **Eggs** • LIVED **?Late Jurassic–Early Cretaceous 150–100 million years ago**

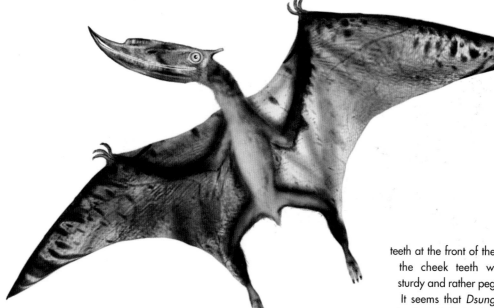

Pterodactyls

Unusual discoveries are quite frequent in the fossil record. New animals and plants continue to surprise scientists with their size and shape. Bizarre creatures are sometimes the norm! Their strangeness often comes about as a result of having to find new and remarkable ways to search for food or to compete for a place to live.

Dsungaripterus certainly looks extraordinary. It was a fairly large pterodactyl with a big head and relatively slim body. A long, low crest ran along the middle of its head from just behind the beaked snout and extended into a prong over the back of its neck. The front of the jaws curved upwards to give the animal a unique appearance. There were no teeth at the front of the jaws but the cheek teeth were very sturdy and rather peg-like.

It seems that *Dsungaripterus* was fond of shellfish: the upturned beak was used to prise the shells from rocks, while the back teeth simply crushed the outer shell to extract the meat from inside.

Pteranodon ter-ran-oh-don

Toothless Flyer

Pterosauria • Pterodactyloidea • Family: Pteranodontidae

FIRST DESCRIBED **1876** • FOUND **North America: USA. Asia: Japan** • WINGSPAN **c.9 m (30 ft)**
• WEIGHT **25 kg (55 lb)** • FOOD **Fish** • YOUNG **Eggs** • LIVED **Late Cretaceous 82–71 million years ago**

Hordes of *Pteranodon* flew over the chalk seas of western America during the Late Cretaceous. They probably nested on cliffs and clifftops well above the water's edge. *Pteranodon* was an odd creature, with its big head crowned by a very large, upright crest. It had long, slightly upturned jaws and no teeth. The crest stabilized the head during flight, and the long jaws were ideal for catching any fish that swam too close to the sea's surface.

Pteranodon had a very small body and its bones were extremely light. They were, in fact, hollow and had very thin walls. It is likely that they were connected to the lungs by a series of air sacs. Those modern seabirds that soar over the oceans on currents of warm air function in the same way.

Pteranodon had small eyes located on the side of the head, towards the back and just below the front of the crest. The 'Toothless Flyer' could not have walked very far on the ground and it is probable that adults simply launched themselves from the cliff edge to go in search of food. Landing must always have been a nightmare, especially in high winds.

Pterodaustro ter-oh-dow-stroh

Wing South

Pterosauria • Pterodactyloidea • Family: Pterodaustridae

FIRST DESCRIBED **1876** • FOUND **South America: Argentina, ?Chile** • WINGSPAN **c.1.3m (4 ft 3 in)** • WEIGHT **8 kg (18 lb)** • FOOD **Pond life** • YOUNG **Eggs** • LIVED **Early Cretaceous 140–125 million years ago**

Pterodaustro was a long-necked, short-tailed pterodactyl with a fairly long head and narrow jaws that curved upwards at the front. The lower jaw was quite strange and had a dense filter on either side. The filters were made up of over a thousand long, 'soft' teeth that resembled the bristles on a brush.

Pterodaustro was a filter-feeder that searched for food in shallow water. It was the Cretaceous equivalent of a flamingo, using the lower jaw as a filter basket into which it probably scooped helpings of water rich in pond life. The water was then forced out through the filter, leaving the tasty morsels behind. Small teeth in the upper and the lower jaws were used to crush the food into smaller pieces.

Pterodaustro was a strong flyer that could take off and land from ground level. It probably fed while on all fours but it would have needed to raise its wings out of the water to take off.

Quetzalcoatlus quet-zal-coh-at-luss

After Quetzalcoatl

Pterosauria • Pterodactyloidea • Family: Azhdarchidae

FIRST DESCRIBED 1971 • FOUND **North America: USA** • WINGSPAN *c*.11 m (36 ft)
• WEIGHT **110 kg (242 lb)** • FOOD **Meat** • YOUNG **Eggs** • LIVED **Late Cretaceous 75–65 million years ago**

Pterodactyls

This gigantic pterosaur was named after the feathered Aztec god Quetzalcoatl. Many pterosaurs are known to have been covered with a furry coat which was rather similar to the soft down found on a modern duck. No feathered pterosaurs have yet been found, however. The fur evolved through the modification of the scaly skin found on most reptiles.

Quetzalcoatlus was the largest animal ever to fly, although it most likely spent much of its time soaring above the mountains like a huge glider. Unlike many pterodactyls, it had very strong wings, with powerful muscles attached to a massively built upper arm bone. It was capable of travelling long distances in search of food. Like *Pterodaustro* (see page 129), *Quetzalcoatlus* was a long-necked pterosaur with individual bones in its back measuring over 30 cm (1 ft) in length. It also had long legs, which would have been very useful when the animal scrambled to feed on the carcass of a dead dinosaur it had spotted from the air.

Quetzalcoatlus and its immediate relatives vanished with the dinosaurs at the end of the Cretaceous period, 65 million years ago. They were the last of the pterosaurs.

Mixosaurus mix-oh-saw-rus

Mixed Lizard

Euryapsida • Ichthyosauria • Family: Mixosauridae

FIRST DESCRIBED **1887** • FOUND **Worldwide** • LENGTH **c.1 m (3 ft 3 in)** • WEIGHT **60 kg (132 lb)** • FOOD **Fish** • YOUNG **Eggs** • LIVED **Middle Triassic 242–230 million years ago**

Although the dinosaurs ruled the land for over 150 million years, the seas were dominated by two very different groups of reptiles. The first of these were the ichthyosaurs or 'fish lizards', which superficially looked like sharks or dolphins. Their shape was perfect for their way of life. *Mixosaurus* was a typical example of an early or primitive 'fish lizard'. It had a long, narrow snout, beautifully streamlined body and long tail. The jaws were armed with dozens of peg-like teeth, and the eyes were very large. *Mixosaurus* was an excellent swimmer, powered by its four strong but relatively short paddles. It did not have the fish-like tail that is found in later types of ichthyosaur.

Mixosaurus is a link between its land-based ancestors and the highly developed ichthyosaurs of Late Triassic and Jurassic times.

Mixosaurus and its immediate relatives were very successful and evidence of them is found throughout the world. They occupied the oceans for nearly 12 million years. Unlike the dinosaurs, Mixosaurs never came on to land so their eggs hatched inside the mother, who then gave birth to live young.

Ichthyosaurs/Mixosaurs

Ophthalmosaurus op-thal-moh-saw-rus
Eye Lizard

Euryapsida • Ichthyosauria • Family: Ophthalmosauridae

FIRST DESCRIBED 1874 • FOUND Europe: England, France, Germany; South America: Argentina; North America: USA • LENGTH *c*.3.5 m (11 ft 6 in) • WEIGHT 1 t • FOOD Fish, squids • YOUNG Live young • LIVED Late Jurassic 160–146 million years ago

By the Late Jurassic, the 'fish lizards' had developed many features that the primitive mixosaurs lacked. *Ophthalmosaurus* was a medium-sized ichthyosaur with a beautifully streamlined body. It had a large fish-type tail and very large eyes. Like dolphins and sharks, it had a vertical dorsal fin on its back. The fin was made of skin and soft body tissue and helped stabilize the animal as it swam along.

Ophthalmosaurus was a very fast, agile swimmer that spent most of its time hunting for food. It lived on small to medium-sized fish and probably dived deep into the oceans in search of squid, cuttlefish and small octopus. *Ophthalmosaurus*, or 'Eye Lizard', could see its prey in very low light. It had eye sockets over 10 cm (4 in) in diameter and the eye was supported by a ring of bone that prevented it from collapsing under pressure when the animal dived deep. All

ichthyosaurs had lungs, so that *Ophthalmosaurus* had to return to the surface for air.

During the Mesozoic (Triassic, Jurassic and Cretaceous), gigantic ichthyosaurs, such as *Shonisaurus sikanniensis*, ruled the oceans of the world. *Shonisaurus* was over 15 m (50 ft) long and weighed around 40 tonnes.

Kronosaurus crone-oh-saw-rus

Krono's Lizard

Euryapsida • Sauropterygia • Pliosauria • Family: Dolichorhynchopidae

FIRST DISCOVERED **1901** • FOUND **Australasia: Australia** • LENGTH **c.12 m (40 ft)** • WEIGHT **50 t** • FOOD **Meat**
• YOUNG **Live young** • LIVED **Early Cretaceous 112 million years ago**

The pliosaurs and plesiosaurs formed the second group of reptiles that flourished in the oceans during the Mesozoic era. Of the two, the pliosaurs had massive heads and short necks, whereas the plesiosaurs had very small heads and long, flexible necks.

Kronosaurus was a typical pliosaur and has been described as one of the most fearsome animals to have lived on Earth. Its enormous head was over 3 m (10 ft) long, with massive jaws and peg-like front teeth of up to 25 cm (10 in) in length. At the back of the jaws the teeth were rounded and it is likely that they were used for crushing shells or bones.

Kronosaurus had four large paddle-like limbs that enabled it to propel itself through water at great speed. In contrast to the long-necked plesiosaurs, the four paddles were roughly the same size, each measuring close to 1 m (3 ft 3 in) in length. It fed on anything, with large fish, reptiles and giant invertebrates (animals without backbones) high on its list of prey.

Ichthyosaurs/Mixosaurs

Elasmosaurus ee-las-moh-saw-rus

Thin-plated Lizard

Euryapsida • Sauropterygia • Plesiosauria • Family: Elasmosauridae

FIRST DISCOVERED **1868** • **Found North America: USA** • LENGTH **c.14 m (46 ft)** • WEIGHT **25 t**
• FOOD **Fish, sea life** • YOUNG **Live young** • LIVED **Late Cretaceous 70–65 million years ago**

Elasmosaurus was a plesiosaur. Unlike *Kronosaurus* (see page 133), it had a small head, a very long neck and a large, barrel-shaped body. It was a gigantic creature; the mysterious Loch Ness Monster is thought to be of similar proportions and may well have been modelled upon it.

The neck accounted for half the dinosaur's total length and was made up of 75 or 76 vertebrae. In comparison, humans have only seven. It was very flexible, although it would have been held in a straight line when the Elasmosaurus was swimming quickly. Plesiosaur paddles were huge structures, with the fingers and toes again accounting for half of their total length. Like turtles, plesiosaurs 'flew' through water, but instead of rotating their paddles in a figure-of-eight movement, as turtles do, they used more of a rowing action.

Whereas *Kronosaurus* lunged at its food, *Elasmosaurus* would have cruised among shoals of fish and ammonites, picking off anything that swam within range. Its small head was armed with numerous conical teeth that effectively interlocked to give greater grip. The *Elasmosaurus* was the longest plesiosaur known from the fossil record.

Ichthyosaurs/Mixosaurs

Protostega pro-toh-stay-gah
First Roof

Anapsida • Chelonia • Family: Protostegidae

FIRST DESCRIBED 1872 • FOUND **North America: USA** • LENGTH *c*.2 m (6 ft 6 in) • WEIGHT **200 kg (440 lb)**
• FOOD **Jellyfish** • YOUNG **Eggs** • LIVED **Late Cretaceous 70–65 million years ago**

In the United States scientists use the term turtle to describe tortoises, terrapins and marine turtles. All tortoises and turtles have a shell that is mostly bony with a covering of horny plates. Many forms can withdraw the head, tail and limbs into their shell for protection but the sea turtles cannot do this. *Protostega* was an ocean-dwelling turtle that lived in the Cretaceous inland sea of western North America.

Like the modern leathery turtle, *Protostega* only came on to land when it laid its eggs. It was perfectly suited to a life at sea and the hard bony shell found in tortoises had been dramatically reduced to save weight. The skull of *Protostega* was quite solid compared to those of birds or dinosaurs. It narrowed towards the front and had a very sharp beak. Only very primitive turtles had teeth. Evidence of deep bite marks on sea turtles such as *Protostega* reveals that sharks were their main enemies.

Turtles

Archelon ark-el-on

Large Turtle

Anapsida • Chelonia • Family: Protostegidae

FIRST DISCOVERED **1897** • FOUND **North America: USA** • LENGTH *c.* **4 m (13 ft)**
• WEIGHT **400 kg (880 lb)** • FOOD **Jellyfish** • YOUNG **Eggs** • LIVED **Late Cretaceous 70–65 million years ago**

Turtles

Archelon is the largest sea turtle on record. It was the size of a rowing boat and was propelled by two huge front paddles. It belonged to the same family as *Protostega* (see page 135) but its bony shell was even thinner and lighter, with large spaces between the ribs and spiny, star-shaped plates replacing the complete bony undershell found in tortoises. *Archelon* would have had a thick outer protective coat made of leathery skin.

Archelon had a very large head and large mouth. Strangely, the beak and the edges of the jaw were not as sharp as those of *Protostega* but the beak was hooked and the roof of the mouth was very robust. So *Archelon* had a vicious bite and the hooked beak would have stopped food from dropping out of its mouth as it was crushed.

Archelon lived in dangerous times. On land the dinosaurs ruled and it is likely that some of the smaller dinosaurs feasted on baby turtles as they left the nest. At sea, sharks would attack juveniles and young adults, but the biggest threat was from the fearsome mosasaurs, giant marine lizards that dominated the seas during the Late Cretaceous.

Metriorhynchus met-ri-oh-rin-kuss

Moderate Snout

Diapsida • Archosauromorpha • Crocodylomorpha • Eusuchia • Family Metriorhynchidae

FIRST DISCOVERED 1838 • FOUND Europe: England, France; South America: Chile • LENGTH c.3 m (10 ft)
• WEIGHT 300 kg (660 lb) • FOOD Fish • YOUNG Eggs • LIVED Middle Jurassic 82–72 million years ago

Metriorhynchus, a strange-looking crocodile, was quite small, with a fish-like tail. The back legs were longer than the front and all four limbs were quite short. Hands and feet were webbed and from this we can tell that *Metriorhynchus* lived a watery lifestyle, prowling the seas of the Middle Jurassic in search of prey. It had a slim body and its head had a box-shaped area around the eyes from which a long, thin snout stuck out. Its teeth were thin and sharp, ideal for eating fish.

Metriorhynchus was not the swiftest and most elegant swimmer of the day, and it probably spent much of its time basking near the surface. It was not armoured and could have been a target for larger ichthyosaurs or giant sharks. Because it spread across the area between Europe and South America, however, it must have been reasonably successful.

Marine crocodiles were like odd blips in the course of evolution. Today's crocodiles have evolved to occupy areas around lakes and rivers. They live in warm climates and feed on all sorts of animal life. They lay eggs and protect their nests and hatchlings. It is hard to imagine *Metriorhynchus* struggling ashore to lay eggs.

Crocodiles

Deinosuchus dye-no-soo-kus

Terrible Crocodile

Diapsida • Archosauromorpha • Crocodylomorpha • Eusuchia • Family: Crocodylidae

FIRST DISCOVERED **1909** • FOUND **North America: USA** • LENGTH *c.*12 m (39 ft) • WEIGHT **3 t**
• FOOD **Meat** • YOUNG **Eggs** • LIVED **Late Cretaceous 82–72 million years ago**

The Age of the Dinosaurs seems to have had more than its fair share of giant meat eaters. The theropods were terrifying and, with gigantic pterosaurs patrolling the skies and fearsome mosasaurs menacing the oceans, nowhere was safe. And if these weren't enough, add one of the world's largest crocodiles skulking on the river bank and life becomes a nightmare world.

Deinosuchus was a huge creature with a 2-m-long (6 ft 6 in) skull and about a hundred large teeth. The teeth were very sturdy and the front, or incisor, teeth were razor sharp. Towards the back of the jaws the teeth were made for crushing.

Deinosuchus was a four-legged monster with a long tail. Normally, it would lie in wait in shallow water or rest on the river bank, but in attack it was a powerful swimmer. It could even lift its body and outrun unsuspecting prey over short distances.

The discovery of *Sarcosuchus imperator* (meaning 'Flesh Crocodile Emperor') in Niger, West Africa, in 1996, challenged the position of *Deinosuchus* as the world's largest-ever crocodile. Whichever was the winner, both probably ate dinosaurs.

Tylosaurus tie-loh-saw-rus

Swollen Lizard

Diapsida • Squamata • Lepidosauria • Family: Mosasauridae

FIRST DISCOVERED **1911** • FOUND **North America: USA; Australasia: New Zealand** • LENGTH **c.15 m (50 ft)**
• WEIGHT **10 t** • FOOD **Sea life** • YOUNG **Live young** • LIVED **Late Cretaceous 85–68 million years ago**

Tylosaurus was a huge sea lizard or mosasaur. It was a distant cousin of the snakes and lizards of today and was a truly terrifying creature, the killing machine of the Late Cretaceous seas. Mosasaurs had huge heads with heavy jaws and dozens of long, sharp, conical teeth. The jaws were loosely joined, allowing for great flexibility and a very wide gape. Modern snakes can swallow animals much larger than themselves, and the big mouth of *Tylosaurus* suggests that it could soon devour a large turtle or very big fish. It also ate ammonites, spiral-shelled Cretaceous relatives of our *Nautilus*, a living spiral-shelled creature.

Unlike the plesiosaurs, *Tylosaurus* had a short neck that merged with a very long, streamlined body. The tail was long and deep, and flattened at the sides. *Tylosaurus* had fairly small paddles which it used to steer, rather than propel itself through the water. Powerful sideways flexes of the body and tail drove the animal towards its prey.

Tylosaurus and the mosasaurs were successful for only a short period of time. But the 'Swollen Lizard' seems to have occupied a territory of many hundreds of miles.

Mosasaurs

Figures in *italics* indicate captions. Main references to dinosaurs are indicated in **bold** type.

Index

Author acknowledgements

I dedicate this book to Boo.

I wish to acknowledge the dedicated help of Neil Curtis
and the continued encouragement of Ross Sandman.

Picture acknowledgements

Alamy/Chris Howes/Wild Places Photography 12
Corbis UK Ltd/Bettmann 9; /Louie Psihovos 13
Science Photo Library/George Bernard 8

Executive Editor Trevor Davies
Editors Alice Bowden, Lisa John
Executive Art Editor Darren Southern
Designer Splinter Group
Picture Library Manager Jennifer Veall
Senior Production Controller Ian Paton